30-MINUTE MENUS

Also by Antony Worrall Thompson

Modern Bistrot Cookery
Supernosh
The Small and Beautiful Cookbook

30-MINUTE MENUS

ANTONY WORRALL THOMPSON

PHOTOGRAPHS BY STEVE LEE

HEADLINE

First published in 1995
by HEADLINE BOOK PUBLISHING

10 9 8 7 6 5 4 3 2 1

British Library Cataloguing in Publication Data

Thompson, Antony Worrall
30-minute Menus
I. Title
641.555

ISBN 0-7472-1472-7 (hardback)
ISBN 0-7472-7810-5 (softback)

Designed by Design/Section
Printed and bound in Italy by Canale & C.S.p.A

HEADLINE BOOK PUBLISHING
A division of Hodder Headline PLC
338 Euston Road
London NW1 3BH

CONTENTS

To Jacinta

ACKNOWLEDGEMENTS

The biggest thank you must go to *The Sunday Times'* readers who have written to me demanding that I write this book. In one voice they were all complaining that their fridge doors were overloaded with magnetic bits holding my *Sunday Times* 30-Minute Menus. So rather than you all buying new fridges, here's the book.

Then, of course there's the team on the 'Style' section of *The Sunday Times*, Alison MacDonald, Tina Moran and Rachel Cooke, who wait with baited breath for my weekly copy, understanding the problem a restaurateur has producing it on time. Originally, copy date was on the Monday preceding the Sunday, then it went back to the previous Friday, Thursday and now Wednesday – they're getting to know me.

To Luisa Alves, until recently my P.A., who badgered me week in, week out for my weekly offering. This was all too much for her, so she resigned to take the easier role as my manager at Bistrot 190. She now gives out to others what she used to take from me.

To her successor, mad fool that she is, Marie-Regine Astic, who takes a firmer hand than Luisa when demanding results. M-R has seen me through nearly half the book never seen by *Sunday Times'* readers. (P.S. She used to be a manager at 190. I think she thought P.A. would be an easier role to handle – now she knows.)

To Steve Lee who photographed the dishes in the book in record time. My instructions to him were simple: 'I don't want the food to look poncy. I want you to get into the middle of the dishes, showing the readers textures, colour and taste ... you know what I mean. I want the reader salivating, licking his lips ...' I think he's done a marvellous job.

To Alan Brooke, Publishing Director, and Celia Kent, Managing Editor of Headline, gluttons for punishment, after all they came back for more after publishing *Modern Bistrot Cookery* last year. Thank you both for your support.

To Susan Fleming, my editor, who has a knack of taking gobbledygook and making it sound like correct English.

To all my staff in all the restaurants, especially Francesca, Mark, Sam, Artie, Max, Harry, Chris, Matthew, Michelle, Graham, Andrew and Adrian, without whom I wouldn't have the time to complete all these other hobbies.

To Sandy Singh, my Chief Executive, who has supported me 100 per cent in my ambitions to create one of the larger restaurant groups in London.

To Fiona Lindsay and Linda Shanks, my agents, who do their best to double my workload every year, and very good they are, too.

And finally to the most exciting person in my life, to whom I have dedicated this book, Jacinta Shiel. She has kept me sane, inspired me, watered and fed me, tasted recipes, put up with my workaholic weekends and generally been an exceptional person.

INTRODUCTION

It was an exciting day when Fiona Lindsay, my literary agent, telephoned me to say *The Sunday Times* wanted me to write 30-Minute Menus for the 'Style' section. Every newspaper has its following but *The Sunday Times* is still king of the Sundays. During Andrew Neil's reign as editor he changed the paper beyond recognition. A great batch of excellent journalists were stolen, borrowed or bought from other sources; headlines became dramatic, content controversial. I guess it wasn't as intellectual as in bygone times, but you could always guarantee a laugh, an eyebrow raised in disbelief, a shiver down the spine, the licking of the lips from the food pages and a knowing chuckle from Craig Brown and, subsequently, A.A. Gill. This was *the* newspaper; this was one of my dreams come true.

That was two years ago and, during that time, I've written a series of seasonal menus, capable of being cooked in 30 minutes. You may say, 'Well, a chef may be able to do it in 30 minutes, but can I?' The answer is yes, if you prepare yourself well before you start to cook. While one dish is cooking, you should be preparing the other. You will find there is preparation to be done in the list of ingredients, e.g. '1 onion, finely chopped', so prepare these items first. Obviously, if you are just starting off on your cookery adventures, you are going to require a little more time but, given the right amount of practice, cooking in half an hour is achievable.

As with any form of job or recreation, cooking is all about confidence and spontaneity. Travel to the market or supermarket, spot some ingredients and think to yourself, 'That'll go well with that: a few fresh herbs, a touch of spice, maybe a little diced shallot instead of onion for a milder flavour...'. Another day you might fancy socking yourself in the mouth with a flavour of the Orient: a dice of chilli, a grating of ginger, some fresh coriander leaves and, of course, the garlic, all fried together with a touch of sesame oil. Experimenting or playing with food is great fun, often creating the best dishes. The only trouble is that unless you write the recipe down at the time you'll curse yourself the next time you want to recreate the same flavours. Remember to taste your food as you go along, don't put too many flavours together, and follow the rule: you can always add, but you can rarely take away.

I've included in this book my favourite recipes from *The Sunday Times* as well as bundles of new ones. It's always encouraging to receive letters from readers, a great many of them have asked me when I was going to produce the book. Well, here it is, recipes from all eras, from all parts of the world. I've got to come clean, I've picked up a lot of ideas from my travels, and from reading my collection of 2,000 cookbooks. I challenge any chef to say that any of his dishes are original; ideas and combinations can be original, but if you read a lot of books or eat out extensively you'll always spot where the inspiration stemmed from. So what? Life is about learning, borrowing, stealing, combining and producing, and so is cooking. In the same way, you'll look at one of the recipes in this book and say, 'Now if I was to add a little of that, or a soupçon of this, I think it would make a better dish.' Good for you; that's cooking, that's fun.

The food you can buy today in supermarkets and specialist shops is unbelievable. Recently I've spotted galangal, lime leaves, ten different kinds of chillies, many different varieties of soy, unusual fresh fish, exciting cuts of meat and a vast array of other ingredients too large to mention. These are exciting times. Not only are we teased in the supermarkets with formerly unknown foodstuffs, subjected to a myriad of food columns in the weekend papers, captivated by exciting colours in the monthlies and brainwashed by food on the radio, but we can also enjoy up to thirty programmes a week on food and wine on network and satellite TV. Chefs have had celebrity status for many years now and I for one get a great kick out of it. How long will this cookery cult last? Who knows? All I'm prepared to do is enjoy it while I can. There will always be those who say 'get back to the kitchen' – that is their right – but while there is a demand from the public, I'll try to satisfy it. My current favourite is *Ready, Steady, Cook*, a fun but nevertheless informative cookery game show that, with audiences of up to 3.5 million, seems to have achieved cult status. You never know what the future holds.

In *30-Minute Menus* I've tried to divide the recipes into seasons, but this is broad based. Most products can be bought all year round but there's something very special about buying the first asparagus in May, eating the first English strawberry in June and savouring tomatoes in summer that have actually been kissed by the sun rather than reared in hot houses. We seem to have forgotten the seasons somewhat, and it's time to reintroduce them. I don't care what they say, there's nothing better than British foods eaten at the right time of year. We've got the products, we must learn to appreciate them. The days of boasting to your friends that you just paid a fortune for the tiniest vegetables from California are over, they didn't taste of anything anyway. Hold on to your money and where possible buy British. Why buy tasteless Golden Delicious apples from France when you can buy a wonderful Cox's Orange Pippin from over here? Why buy crated veal from Holland when British 'Rose' veal reared in humane conditions is just as good? Have you discovered the white meat alternative, pork, a much maligned meat that is excellent value? No, then it's time for the Government to spend more money on promoting all that's good about Britain.

What you've got here is a collection of user-friendly food thoughts and simple menus;

nothing pompous, nothing for the foodie purist. I can't be doing with pleasing such a small minority of the British public. Life's too short to worry about whether it's politically or morally correct to combine certain tastes. I couldn't give a damn whether somebody's going to get upset because I've combined Northern Italy with Southern France, or mixed Far Eastern spices with Indian spices. Cooking should be fun and, if that means mixing and matching and you're happy with the result, then that's all that counts. Have fun, enjoy your playtime and, most importantly, relax. The best cooking and the best entertaining occur if you're at ease with yourself; this happens if you're in charge, fully prepared, and for many of us, slightly lubricated with the odd glass of wine ... or two!

Most of the recipes are for two or four people but can usually be multiplied up or divided down depending on your requirements. Most of the ingredients are easy to find, especially now that the large supermarket chains have introduced specialist foods sections into many of their branches. I've deliberately made the recipes approachable with no hidden 'cheffie' tricks; everything is there for you to produce without needing a huge depth of cooking skills.

The main thing is to have fun, mix and match, play and experiment, and always approach cookery with one thought in mind: 'This is going to be great, I'm going to enjoy myself and the food will be delicious.' Since it's so personal I've left seasoning down to you, so many of the recipes state 'season to taste'. Taste is the operative word; if you taste during all the stages of the cooking, you shouldn't have a problem. Don't let cooking become a burden; if it does, then you've got the wrong hobby and you'd do better eating in one of my restaurants or picking up the phone for a take-away! Good luck, not that you'll need it!

SPRING MENUS

KICK START YOUR DAY
Caribbean Smoothie
Muesli with Pineapple Cream
Kedgeree

BRIDGING THE GAP
Chicken Liver Pâté
Melba Toast
Deep-fried Camembert

PURE SIMPLICITY
Rocket, Chicory and Parmesan Salad
Spaghettini with Turbot, Breadcrumbs and Parsley

MASTERING THE MED
Tortino
Chargrilled Squid with Marinated Red Chicory

PASS THE POLENTA
Quail Saltimbocca with Gorgonzola Polenta
Fritters with Raisins and Marsala

UNDERSTANDING BROCCOLI
Warm Broccoli Salad
Fiery Rice

FOOD WITHOUT FASHION
Herb Soup
Unfashionable 'Steak au Poivre'

TWO USES FOR A CAN OPENER
Sardine and Potato Salad
Tinned Salmon Balls

FISHING FOR COMPLIMENTS
Baked Eggs with Potted Shrimps
Herbed Trout with Fennel

BRUNCH POWER
Potato Cakes with Smoked Salmon
and Soured Cream
Bloody Rabbit

THE POWER BREAKFAST
Carrot Cocktail
Egg-white Omelette with Asparagus and Herbs

CLASSIC COMBO	Egg Mousse with Smoked Cod's Roe
	Calf's Liver and Bacon
A TRIBUTE TO ELIZABETH DAVID	Watercress and Potato Soup
	Piperade
TEA WITH GRAIN	Cream Cheese and Cucumber
	Egg, Pistachio and Basil
	Herby Fruit Salad
BORN FOR BEER	Pickled Herring Salad
	Chicken in a Mexican Nutty Herb Sauce
	Chilli-fried Potatoes
LEARNING TO LIVE WITH LEFTOVERS	Asparagus, Smoked Bacon and Spring Onion Hash
	Roast Lamb Salad on a Potato Cake
SEDUCING THE SEASONS	Last-of-the-Season Leek and First-of-the-Season Pea Soup
	Mediterranean Squid and Vegetable Casserole
GRATEFULLY IRISH	White Soda Bread or Rolls
	Mussels with Bacon
CHECKING OUT THE CHILLI	Chicken, Chilli and Corn Soup
	Grilled Mackerel with Chilli and Horseradish
HAPPY TO BE HEALTHY	Scallops with Green Mango
	Soup Noodles
EGGS FOR BREAKFAST	Sunday Morning Kick-start
	Egg on Egg Omelette
	Crispy-fried Tomatoes
A TOUCH OF SPICE	Tandoori Chicken Salad
	Spicy Fish Curry

BREAKFAST MEETS LUNCH	Poached Eggs with Parma Ham and Mushrooms Chopped Peppered Lamb Steak
LUNCH ON A BUDGET	Potato Salad with Mollet Eggs Wine-pickled Mackerel
PROUD TO BE BRITISH	Asparagus with Soft-boiled Eggs and Burnt Butter Rare Beef Salad Strawberries with Rum
EASTER FOR TWO	Turkey with Poached Eggs and Tarragon Mustard Sauce Melted Mars Bars over Ice Cream
THE ALTERNATIVE EASTER	Tuna Tartare Rolled in Soft Herbs Tartare of 'Rose' Veal with Parmesan 'Tartare' of Celeriac Rémoulade
SPRING HAS SPRUNG	Salad of Asparagus with Avocado and Walnuts Fruit Salad with Kiwi Juices
MEMORIES OF WINTER	Oystered Asparagus Schnuggies in a Skillet
BREAKING FOR SUMMER	Cold Pea Soup with Scallops, Mint and Sorrel Mussel Sate with Ginger and Coconut
NEW-SEASON FARE	A Salad of Goat's Cheese, Peas and Broad Beans New-season Lamb with Asparagus and New Potatoes

KICK START YOUR DAY

(SERVES 2)

Somerset Maugham once said, 'To eat well in England you should have breakfast three times a day.' Nowadays you can toss that quote out with the dishwater for, as we all know, you can eat brilliantly in England at other times of the day as well. But he had a point, breakfast is an excellent part of life's culinary diary – if you've got the energy, that is. Fresh juices, fruits and then on to an energy-giving carbohydrate dish such as a steaming bowl of kedgeree.

Caribbean Smoothie

½ pineapple, peeled, cored and cubed
2 bananas, peeled and chopped
¾ pint (450 ml) unsweetened coconut milk
2 tbsp bran
ice cubes

Push the pineapple through a centrifugal juicer, set aside the juice and retain the pulp for the next dish. Blend the banana, coconut milk, bran and pineapple juice with a few ice cubes in a liquidiser until smooth. Pour into two tall glasses. Garnish with an umbrella, a plastic monkey and palm-tree stirrer, if in the mood.

Muesli with Pineapple Cream

¾ pint (450 ml) dry flat cider
2 tbsp Calvados
4 tbsp pineapple pulp (see above)
2 tbsp liquid honey
4 tbsp double cream
6 oz (175 g) your favourite muesli

Combine the cider, Calvados, pineapple and honey in a saucepan and cook over a medium heat until the liquid is reduced to ½ pint (300 ml). Add the cream. If it is a cold day, pour hot over the muesli and combine; if it's warm weather, allow the liquid to cool first. Adjust the sweetness with more honey if required.

Kedgeree

1 kipper fillet
6 oz (175 g) fresh salmon fillet
⅓ pint (300 ml) double cream
1 bay leaf
½ onion, chopped
2 oz (50 g) unsalted butter
1 tsp curry paste
8 oz (225 g) cooked rice
2 hard-boiled eggs, chopped
2 tbsp chopped parsley
salt and ground black pepper

Cook the fishes in the cream with the bay leaf over a medium heat for 7 minutes, then allow to cool slightly. Discard the bay leaf, reserve the cream and flake the fish, discarding any skin or bone. Meanwhile, cook the onion slowly in the butter until soft but not browned, add the curry paste and stir to combine. Add the rice, flaked fish, hard-boiled eggs and parsley and stir. Add enough of the reserved cream to make the mixture unctuous, then season to taste and serve immediately.

BRIDGING THE GAP

(SERVES 2–4)

I'm always looking for nibbles — snack food has a sense of naughtiness about it. A quick chicken liver pâté is useful and, to go with that, how about some melba toast which can be made well in advance and stored in a sealed plastic container. Another dish that we all love but are scared of owning up to (a bit like Hello magazine) is deep-fried Camembert.

Chicken Liver Pâté

1 oz (25 g) softened butter
8 oz (225 g) chicken livers, cleaned
½ pint (300 ml) milk
3 egg yolks
1 shallot, finely diced
1 clove garlic, finely diced
1 tsp soft thyme leaves
salt and ground black pepper
1 oz (25 g) soft breadcrumbs

Preheat the oven to 160°C/325°F/Gas 3 and grease four small moulds with butter. Put the livers, milk, egg yolks, shallot, garlic and thyme in the food processor and blend until smooth. Season with salt and black pepper. Pass through a fine sieve and then add the breadcrumbs. Pour the mixture into the moulds and then place in a roasting tray. Add hot water to the tray to come three-quarters of the way up the sides of the moulds. Cook in the oven until the pâté has set, about 20 minutes. Eat hot or cold with pickle, chutney and melba toast.

Melba Toast

sliced white bread, thin cut

Under a grill toast thin slices of ordinary white bread on both sides until light golden. Cut off the crusts and cut each slice of toast horizontally between the toasted faces, leaving you with very thin slices of bread toasted on one side. Grill the untoasted sides very briefly until crisp, golden and slightly curly. Cool and store in a sealed plastic container.

Deep-fried Camembert

8 individual portions ripe Camembert
plain flour for coating
2 eggs, beaten
fresh uncoloured breadcrumbs
salt and cayenne pepper
oil for deep-frying

Coat each piece of cheese first in flour, then dip in the egg, and coat them in breadcrumbs. Season with salt and cayenne pepper. Rest in the freezer for 15 minutes. Deep-fry in vegetable oil until golden, about 1 minute. Serve with cranberry sauce, gooseberry relish or your favourite chutney.

PURE SIMPLICITY

(SERVES 2)

Sometimes chefs find it hard to create really simple food but, after two years of writing for The Sunday Times, it is getting easier. When purity grabs me, I seek simplicity at its best and then I turn to a 'simple' salad, free from the rigours of herbs or any form of composition. I love rocket and, when these peppery leaves are mixed with bitter leaves, you end up with the following Rocket, Chicory and Parmesan Salad: the Parmesan is the foil between the two other flavours. Follow that with a pasta – Spaghettini with Turbot, Breadcrumbs and Parsley.

Rocket, Chicory and Parmesan Salad

2 handfuls rocket, washed and dried
1 head chicory, split into leaves
salt and ground black pepper
4 tbsp extra virgin olive oil
2 oz (50 g) good Parmesan (Parmigiano Reggiano), shaved into curls with a vegetable peeler
2 lemon wedges

Remove any thick stems from the rocket. Place them in a salad bowl. Rip the chicory into bite-sized pieces and add to the rocket. Sprinkle the sides of the bowl with salt and ground black pepper (by doing this the seasoning doesn't stick to the individual leaves). Drizzle the leaves with the olive oil. Toss gently. Arrange the Parmesan flakes on top and serve with the wedges of lemon.

Spaghettini with Turbot, Breadcrumbs and Parsley

10 oz (275 g) dried spaghettini
2 tbsp olive oil
1 clove garlic, finely chopped
pinch dried chilli flakes
pinch dashi soup powder (optional)
4 tinned anchovy fillets, drained
2 oz (50 g) fresh breadcrumbs
10 oz (275 g) turbot fillet, cut into 1-in (2.5-cm) cubes (any other white fish can be substituted)
salt and ground black pepper
2 tbsp chopped flat parsley leaves
1 tbsp extra virgin olive oil
2 tsp lemon juice

Cook the pasta in plenty of boiling water until *al dente*, about 8-10 minutes. Heat the olive oil in a frying pan, add the garlic, chilli, dashi powder and anchovy fillets and cook, stirring regularly, until the anchovies have disintegrated. Add the breadcrumbs and fry until golden. Add the fish and stir-fry over a high heat for about 5 minutes or until the fish is just cooked. Drain the pasta and mix with the fish mixture. Season to taste. Mix in the parsley, drizzle with extra virgin olive oil and lemon juice, and serve immediately.

MASTERING THE MED

(SERVES 4)

The Spanish and the Italians seem to do more exciting things with eggs than us Brits. But, having said that, they would probably find our scrambled eggs a little different. Spanish tortillas and Italian frittatas sound a little more romantic than boiled eggs with toasted 'soldiers'. A dish I enjoy is the Italian tortino which is similar to the tortilla but cooked in the oven. Chargrilled Squid with Marinated Red Chicory makes an exciting follow-up to the eggs.

Tortino

8 oz (225 g) asparagus, cut into 1-in (2.5-cm) pieces
salt and ground black pepper
1 shallot, finely diced
1 oz (25 g) unsalted butter
2 handfuls spinach, thick stems removed
1 tsp soft thyme leaves
5 large eggs, beaten
1 tbsp milk
3 tbsp freshly grated Parmesan

Preheat the oven to 200°C/400°F/Gas 6. Blanch the asparagus in boiling salted water for 3 minutes, then plunge into cold water to arrest the cooking. Drain. Pan-fry the shallot in half the butter until soft but not brown, then add the spinach and thyme leaves and cook until the leaves have wilted. Squeeze the liquid from the spinach and transfer the drained mixture to a buttered shallow baking dish. Top the spinach with the asparagus. Combine the eggs, milk, Parmesan and seasoning and pour over the vegetables. Lift the vegetables to allow the egg to cover the bottom of the dish. Place in the oven and cook for about 15 minutes or until the eggs are set. This dish can be eaten hot or at room temperature.

Chargrilled Squid with Marinated Red Chicory

1½ pints (900 ml) water
½ pint (300 ml) cider vinegar
1½ oz (40 g) caster sugar
1 tsp salt
1 chilli, sliced in two
1 sprig thyme
1 bay leaf
1 tsp crushed black pepper corns
1 tsp crushed juniper berries
4 heads red chicory
½ pint (200 ml) extra virgin olive oil
6 tbsp chopped flat parsley leaves
salt and ground black pepper
1 lb (450 g) squid, cleaned
1 tsp chilli oil

Bring the first nine ingredients to the boil in a non-reactive saucepan. Add the chicory to the marinade and cook for a further 10 minutes. Drain well, allow to cool, then cover the chicory with the oil and scatter with parsley. Season to taste. Allow to marinate for as long as possible. (The chicory can be eaten immediately but will keep up to 5 days and also makes a good addition to any charcuterie.) Lightly slash the inside of the squid at ½-in (2.5-cm) intervals without cutting all the way through. Not only does the finished result look professional, it also helps the squid to cook through quickly: the shorter the cooking time the more tender the product. Place the squid on the chargrill and cook for no more than 1 minute each side, depending on its thickness. Season and dribble with chilli oil. Serve with the room-temperature chicory.

PASS THE POLENTA

(SERVES 4)

Polenta raises fierce debate as to whether it was a fashionable trend never to be seen again or whether one of Italy's staple foods will stay with us as part of the new Mediterranean diet. This menu also contains the use of another debatable item, the quail, which for some is a waste of space. Moi, I think it's a great snacking bird, so it's Quail Saltimbocca with Gorgonzola Polenta followed by Fritters with Raisins and Marsala.

Quail Saltimbocca with Gorgonzola Polenta

8 quail, spatchcocked (split down the backbone and flattened)
salt and ground black pepper
16 sage leaves
4 slices prosciutto or Parma ham
1 pint (600 ml) milk
2 oz (50 g) unsalted butter
6 oz (175 g) quick-cook polenta
2 tbsp soured cream
2 oz (50 g) Gruyère cheese, grated
1 oz (25 g) Parmesan, grated
3 oz (75 g) Gorgonzola cheese, crumbled
1 oz (25 g) raisins
pinch nutmeg

Season the quail on both sides with salt and ground black pepper. Top the skin side with two sage leaves and half a slice of prosciutto. Set aside until ready to cook. In a heavy-bottomed saucepan bring the milk and half the butter to the boil. Add the polenta in a thin stream, whisking constantly for about 5 minutes, until the mixture becomes thick and smooth. Fold in the soured cream, Gruyère, Parmesan, Gorgonzola, raisins and a pinch of nutmeg, stirring until smooth. Set aside to keep warm. If you want to fry or grill the polenta, pour the mixture into an oiled shallow roasting tray and smooth with a palette knife. Allow to cool, then cut the polenta into rectangles and fry, grill or chargrill with a little grated cheese and some breadcrumbs scattered on the top. When nearly ready to serve, heat the remaining butter in a large frying pan. Add the quail non-skin-side down and cook for 3 minutes. Place the pan under a pre-heated grill and cook the prosciutto-covered sides of the quail for a further 3 minutes. Serve with the polenta.

Fritters with Raisins and Marsala

2 oz (50 g) raisins
¼ pint (150 ml) Marsala or sweet sherry
8 oz (225 g) plain flour
pinch salt
2 egg yolks
¼ pint (150 ml) milk
vegetable oil for frying
caster sugar for dusting

Soak the raisins in the Marsala for 15 minutes. Drain, reserving the wine. Place the flour and salt in a large mixing bowl, make a well in the centre and gradually add the Marsala, stirring constantly. Stir in the egg yolks and raisins with enough milk to make a batter the consistency of thick cream. In a large frying pan heat 1 in (2.5 cm) of vegetable oil. Using a small ladle or 3 tbsp for each fritter, spoon the batter into the hot oil. Cook three or four at a time for 5 minutes, turning once, then drain on kitchen paper. Repeat until all the batter is used up. Dust with caster sugar and serve hot.

UNDERSTANDING BROCCOLI
(SERVES 4)

Broccoli has become a cliché, I guess, as it is found everywhere, but not many people know that it's packed full of all sorts of healthy things. In fact it does you more good than 90 per cent of vegetables on the market – try the Broccoli and Pear Juice. Anyway, I digress, back to the menu: to start, Warm Broccoli Salad, swiftly followed by Fiery Rice – you can't get much healthier than that.

Warm Broccoli Salad

1 onion, grated
4 anchovy fillets, mashed
2 tsp capers, rinsed and chopped
juice of ½ lemon
3 tbsp extra virgin olive oil
1 tsp chopped mint leaves
10 oz (275 g) broccoli florets
ground black pepper

Combine the onion, anchovy, capers, lemon juice, olive oil and mint in a bowl. In plenty of boiling salted water cook the broccoli for 3 minutes, then drain and toss with the prepared ingredients. Season with black pepper. Serve immediately. This salad can be equally successful served at room temperature.

Fiery Rice

5 tbsp extra virgin olive oil
2 onions, finely diced
2 bay leaves
3 cloves garlic, mashed
1 x 375-g can chopped tomatoes
1 tsp hot chilli flakes
4 tbsp chopped flat parsley
salt and ground black pepper
8 oz (225 g) arborio rice
¼ pint (150 ml) dry white wine
1½ pints (900 ml) vegetable stock, hot
2 oz (50 g) unsalted butter
4 tbsp grated Parmesan

In a medium saucepan, heat half of the olive oil, add half the onion and cook until the onion is soft but not brown. Add the bay leaves, garlic, tomatoes and chilli flakes and cook over a medium heat until the tomato thickens into a sauce. Add the parsley and season to taste. Meanwhile, in a large saucepan over a medium heat, cook the remaining oil and onion for 5 minutes. Add the rice and cook until the rice smells slightly nutty. Add the white wine and stir until it has been absorbed by the rice. Add the stock, ladle by ladle, allowing it to be absorbed before adding more. When the rice is nearly cooked but still *al dente*, add the tomato sauce and cook for a further 5 minutes. Fold in the butter and Parmesan and season to taste. Serve immediately.

FOOD WITHOUT FASHION
(SERVES 2)

Dishes come and go as food fashions are affected by prevailing whims. 'Real' food sticks around forever. One of these dishes is the steak au poivre or peppered steak. The occasional piece of red meat is delicious. I know it's frowned upon, but the media is mainly to blame. Remember my motto: 'Everything in moderation, and a little in excess.' In other words, enjoy yourself, after all, life's too short to worry about every food scare. To start, a bowl of herby soup.

Herb Soup

2 oz (50 g) unsalted butter
1 onion, finely chopped
1 clove garlic, finely chopped
1 bay leaf
1 potato, peeled and diced
4 tbsp chopped lovage leaves
1½ pints (900 ml) vegetable stock
2 tbsp tarragon leaves
1 bunch dill, large stems removed
½ bunch flat parsley, large stems removed
salt and ground black pepper

Heat the butter in a heavy-based saucepan over a medium heat. When the butter is frothing, add the onion, garlic and bay leaf and cook for 5 minutes, stirring regularly. Add the potato and lovage leaves. (If no lovage is available use celery leaves.) Toss to combine, then add the stock, bring to the boil and simmer for 15-20 minutes, or until the potato is cooked. During the last 2 minutes add the tarragon, dill and parsley. Transfer the soup to a liquidiser or food processor and blend for 30 seconds. Return the soup to the saucepan and heat through. Season to taste.

Unfashionable 'Steak au Poivre'

1 lb (450 g) rump steak, cut 2 in/5 cm thick
3 tsp crushed black pepper corns
1 oz (25 g) unsalted butter
2 tbsp brandy
1 tsp French mustard
1 tsp Worcestershire sauce
4 tbsp beef stock
2 tbsp red wine
1 tbsp green peppercorns in brine
4 tbsp double cream
salt to taste

Preheat the oven to 190°C/375°F/Gas 5. Press the cracked pepper into both sides of the steak. Heat a ridged cast iron skillet over a high heat, add the butter and, when foaming, the steak. Cook for 2 minutes on each side. Pop in to the oven and cook for a further 8 minutes if you like your meat rare, longer if required. Remove from the oven and set the meat aside to rest, keeping it warm. Over a medium heat, add the brandy to the skillet, scrape up all the meat juices, then add the mustard, Worcestershire sauce, beef stock and red wine. Whisk to combine, and cook until the sauce has reduced by a third. Pour into the sauce any juices that have seeped from the beef. Add the green peppercorns and cream and cook for a further 2 minutes. Season to taste with salt. Slice the meat at an angle, then arrange on two plates and coat with the sauce. A leaf salad or some buttered leaf spinach and new Jersey mids would be suitable companions.

TWO USES FOR A CAN OPENER
(SERVES 4)

I have to own up to a penchant for some canned goods. In fact my life is sometimes dominated by Heinz, what with their tomato soup, baked beans and vegetable salad — and that's not mentioning the love affair I have with their ketchup. Two of the canned products that find a home in my larder are Alaskan canned salmon and vintage sardines, stored at least ten years before eating and turned lovingly every two months. Here's a couple of quickie recipes that use these two products.

Sardine and Potato Salad

8 oz (225 g) waxy new potatoes
salt and ground black pepper
1 x 120-g can sardines in oil
2 tsp extra virgin olive oil
2 tsp lemon juice
1 tsp Dijon mustard
a handful crisp salad leaves
3 spring onions, sliced
1 tbsp mayonnaise

Boil the new potatoes in salted water until tender. Drain and slice while still warm. While the potatoes are cooking, whisk together the oil from the sardines, the extra virgin olive oil, lemon juice and mustard. Season with salt and ground black pepper. Mix the potatoes with the dressing and set on the crisp salad leaves. Meanwhile bone and mash the sardines and combine with the spring onion, mayonnaise and plenty of black pepper. Serve on top of the warm potato salad.

Tinned Salmon Balls

1 x 213-g can Alaskan salmon
6 oz (175 g) leftover mashed potato
1 oz (25 g) unsalted butter, softened
1 hard-boiled egg, chopped
2 tsp chopped dill
2 tsp chopped parsley
1 tsp salt
½ tsp ground white pepper
2 eggs, beaten
fresh breadcrumbs for coating
vegetable oil for frying

Mash the salmon, crushing the bones with a fork (canned bones are delicious). Mix the salmon with the potato, softened butter, boiled egg, dill, parsley, salt, pepper and half the beaten egg. Flour your hands and shape the mix into balls. Dip them in the remaining beaten egg and coat them in breadcrumbs. Deep-fry in hot oil for 3 minutes. Serve with ketchup (sacreligious), tartare sauce or hot parsley sauce.

FISHING FOR COMPLIMENTS

(SERVES 2)

Here's a menu using two of our most famous 'fishy' products that have recently become mislaid in our constant desire to search for more off-the-wall items. To start, baked eggs with Morecambe Bay potted shrimps (any other bay will do), followed by the extremely good-value trout, stuffed with herbs, roasted and served with fennel.

Baked Eggs with Potted Shrimps

1 x 2-oz tub potted shrimps
salt and ground black pepper
3 fl oz (85 ml) double cream, heated
2 large free-range eggs

Preheat the oven to 190°C/375°F/Gas 5. Butter two china ramekins, using butter from the shrimps. Push half the potted shrimps into the bottom of each ramekin. Season the cream and pour on to the shrimps. Break an egg into each ramekin and place in a small baking dish half-filled with hot water. Bake in the oven for 7–10 minutes, depending on how firm you like your eggs. Serve immediately, with buttered toast 'soldiers'.

Herbed Trout with Fennel

4 sprigs rosemary
4 sprigs fennel top
4 sprigs parsley
4 sprigs oregano
2 x 10–12-oz (400–450-g) trout, gutted
good olive oil
3 tbsp fresh lemon juice
salt and ground black pepper
2 small heads fennel, cut in 2 lengthways
rocket leaves

Preheat the oven to 190°C/375°F/Gas 5. Place the herbs inside the trout and arrange the fish in a shallow baking tray. Pour ¼ pint (150 ml) of olive oil over the fish. Add the lemon juice and season with salt and ground black pepper. Marinade for 10 minutes (longer if possible). Blanch the fennel in salted boiling water for 10 minutes, then drain and place next to the trout. Drain off the marinade and pour a little more olive oil into the baking tray. Brown the trout and fennel over a medium heat on top of the stove, turning once, then place in the oven for approximately 15 minutes to finish cooking, while you eat the baked eggs. Serve the trout with the fennel, a little marinade and a few dressed rocket leaves.

BRUNCH POWER

(SERVES 2)

Perfect for a Sunday supper, or better still a brunch, I kick off with a fairly classic combination of smoked salmon and soured cream, accompanied by crunchy potato cakes and all the trimmings. I haven't a clue where the next dish came from. I think I had one of those brain seizures, not knowing whether I wanted to start with a Bloody Mary or finish with a Welsh rabbit, so you're getting both. Believe it or not, it's actually quite delightful!

Potato Cakes with Smoked Salmon and Soured Cream

8 oz (225 g) large potatoes, peeled and grated
1 tsp thyme leaves
½ onion, grated
1 egg, beaten
2 tbsp rolled oats
2 tbsp crumbled cornflakes
salt and ground black pepper
unsalted butter for frying
6 oz (175 g) Scottish smoked salmon, sliced
1 tbsp small capers
1 tbsp snipped chives
4 tbsp soured cream
½ red onion, sliced
1 lemon, halved

Mix the potatoes with the thyme leaves, onion, eggs, oats and cornflakes. Season to taste and combine well. Heat some butter in a non-stick pan, add large spoonfuls of the potato mixture and fry for 4 minutes each side. Serve the potato cakes with smoked salmon, a scattering of capers and chives, a dollop of soured cream, some sliced onions and lemon halves.

Bloody Rabbit

1 oz (25 g) unsalted butter
½ onion, finely diced
1 oz (25 g) plain flour
1 tsp dry mustard powder
1 tbsp Worcestershire sauce
1 tsp Tabasco sauce
½ pint (300 ml) good tomato juice
3 fl oz (85 ml) vodka
4 oz (100 g) Cheddar cheese, grated
celery salt and ground black pepper
2 slices buttered toast

In a saucepan, melt the butter over a medium heat, add the onion and cook until soft but not brown. Add the flour and cook, stirring constantly, for 2 minutes. Add the mustard powder, Worcestershire and Tabasco sauces. Stir to combine, add the tomato juice and bring to the boil. Simmer until the mixture thickens. Whisk in the vodka and grated Cheddar, and cook until melted. Season to taste and spoon the sauce over the hot toast. If you desire, flash under a hot grill until the cheese is bubbling.

THE POWER BREAKFAST

(SERVES 1)

Researching for my new breakfast menu at 190 Queen's Gate I came across an American habit of eating 'egg-white omelette'. 'Plonkers,' was my initial thought, 'what a waste of egg yolks.' But one's got to try out new ideas and so I sat myself down to a 'power breakfast'. Carrot juice to start, freshly processed in a centrifugal juicer with hints of ginger and celery: delicious, I'm really hooked. This was followed up with the egg-white omelette filled with asparagus and fresh herbs: excellent, who needs yolks anyway? If you are feeling hungry, add a bowl of favourite cereal, enriched with potassium-laden mango and banana, to kick start your morning.

Carrot Cocktail

4 medium carrots, peeled
½ in (1 cm) fresh ginger, peeled
ice cubes, broken
1 stick celery, washed

Feed all the ingredients into your juicer. Pour the resulting vividly shocking orange liquid on to some broken rocks. Serve with an extra stick of celery as an edible garnish.

Egg-white Omelette with Asparagus and Herbs

vegetable oil
3 egg whites (keep yolks for another use)
1 tbsp finely chopped herbs, such as parsley, chives, chervil
salt and ground black pepper
3 asparagus spears, blanched and cut into 1-in (2.5-cm) sections

Heat a tiny amount of oil in a non-stick omelette pan. Beat the egg whites with a fork and add the herbs, salt and ground black pepper. In a seperate pan, toss asparagus in some oil until heated through, then season with salt and ground black pepper. Set aside and keep warm. Pour the egg white into the oiled omelette pan and, with a fork, quickly draw the edges to the centre, so the omelette cooks evenly. When cooked but still creamy, place the asparagus in the centre and leave on the heat for a second longer. With a fork, fold the omelette towards the far lip of the pan, giving the pan a light tap to loosen the omelette. Slide out on to a warm plate.

Potato Salad with Mollet Eggs

Cold Pea Soup with Scallops, Mint and Sorrel

CLASSIC COMBO

(SERVES 4)

Whatever happened to that breed of Londoner called a Sloane? You don't really hear the word mentioned nowadays. Maybe it's time for the sequel 'Sloane Alone II'. In their heyday I remember there was a wonderful 'Sloaney' restaurant called Monkey's in Chelsea Green (still going strong) which served excellent food, particularly a delicious egg mousse with huge amounts of caviar — those dizzy 1980s nights! That was a long time ago, but I think I've reproduced a dish for you in a similar vein. However, we're not really in a caviar era, so I've substituted slices of smoked cod roe. To follow, one of the all-time classics, Calf's Liver and Bacon with a little modern twist.

Egg Mousse with Smoked Cod's Roe

4 hard-boiled eggs, chopped
2 tbsp softened unsalted butter
1 small bunch chives, snipped
3 anchovy fillets, finely chopped
1 tbsp good mayonnaise
1 tbsp soured cream
juice of ½ lemon
ground black pepper
8 oz (225 g) smoked cod's roe

Mix the hard-boiled eggs with the softened butter and chives. Mash the anchovy with the mayonnaise and soured cream. Fold this into the egg mixture. Season with lemon juice and ground black pepper. Place this in a bowl and leave in the refrigerator until ready to eat. Cut the cod's roe in ½-in (1-cm) slices and serve with the mousse, hot toast, and extra soured cream.

Calf's Liver and Bacon

4 slices sweet-cure back bacon, rinds removed
4 slices sweet-cure streaky bacon, rinds removed
2 onions, finely sliced
2 oz (50 g) unsalted butter
1 tbsp good olive oil
4 x 5-oz (150-g) slices calf's liver
salt and ground black pepper
2 tbsp still mineral water
2 tbsp balsamic vinegar

In a large frying pan, cook the bacon without fat, turning once, until the fat is crispy. Remove the bacon and keep warm. In the same pan fry the onions in bacon fat over a moderate heat until soft. Increase the heat and continue cooking until the onions are crispy. Meanwhile, in another pan, melt half the butter with the olive oil over a high heat. Season the liver with salt and ground black pepper and pan-fry for 2-3 minutes each side, depending on how rare you like your liver. Divide the liver, bacon and onions between four warm plates. To the liver pan add the mineral water and balsamic vinegar; bring to the boil, scraping the grungy bits off the bottom. When boiling, add the remaining butter and cook until combined with the juices. Season to taste and spoon over the liver.

A TRIBUTE TO ELIZABETH DAVID
(SERVES 6)

Elizabeth David probably did more to educate the British palate than any other writer this century. I only met her three or four times, cooking for her twice, but the impression she made on me will survive throughout my cooking lifetime. This menu is inspired by two of the first dishes I attempted from her cookbooks, a creamy Watercress and Potato Soup and a Basque dish of eggs and peppers called Piperade, served with Bayonne ham.

Watercress and Potato Soup

2 shallots, finely diced
1 sprig thyme
1oz (25 g) unsalted butter
2 bunches watercress, leaves and stalks separate
1lb (450 g) floury potatoes, peeled and diced
2 pints (1.2 litres) vegetable or chicken stock, boiling
½ pint (300 ml) double cream
salt and ground black pepper

Cook the shallot and thyme gently in the butter until soft but not brown. Add the watercress stalks and potatoes and stir to combine. Add the boiling stock and cook aggressively until the potato is soft. Add half the watercress leaves, cook for a further minute, then liquidise. Pass the puréed soup through a fine sieve. Add the cream and the remaining watercress leaves. Heat through and season to taste.

Piperade

¾ lb (350 g) onion, finely sliced
1 clove garlic, finely diced
1 tsp soft thyme leaves
3 tbsp good olive oil
1 red pepper, seeded and cut into thin strips
1 green pepper, seeded and cut into thin strips
6 tomatoes, peeled and chopped
10 eggs, beaten
salt and ground black pepper
12 oz (350 g) Bayonne or Parma ham, thinly sliced

Whilst the soup is being prepared, cook the onion, garlic and thyme in the olive oil until soft. Add the peppers and cook for 10 minutes. Add the tomatoes and cover the pan. Cook until all the ingredients are soft and combined. (This could be prepared ahead up to this point.) When ready to eat, pour in the eggs and cook as for scrambled eggs. Season to taste and serve hot with slices of ham on the side.

TEA WITH GRAIN

(SERVES 4)

I really used to look forward to afternoon tea with my Gran: thin sandwiches, buttered crumpets, scones with all the trimmings, lardy cake, usually some sort of fruit and, of course, a big pot of Earl Grey tea. But now she's left me to go to that tea room in the sky, things ain't the same, and afternoon tea has become seriously neglected. As it's a British way of life, it should definitely feature in your Sunday afternoon 'enjoyment factor'. I include a couple of sandwich fillings and a herby winter fruit salad.

Cream Cheese and Cucumber

¼ lb (100 g) soft cream cheese
1 tbsp double cream
2 tbsp snipped chives
salt and ground black pepper
4 thin slices wholewheat bread
½ cucumber, thinly sliced
2 tbsp chopped mint

Mix together the cream cheese, double cream and chives. Season to taste. Spread on the slices of bread and top with cucumber slices and chopped mint. Cover with the remaining slice of bread cut into quarters.

Egg, Pistachio and Basil

4 large eggs, hard boiled
2 tbsp chopped pistachios
3 tbsp soured cream
1 tsp Dijon mustard
12 basil leaves, ripped
salt and paprika
4 thin slices wholewheat bread

Chop the hard-boiled eggs and combine with the nuts, soured cream, Dijon mustard and basil. Season to taste and fill the sandwiches as normal.

Herby Fruit Salad

¼ pint (150 ml) unsweetened
coconut milk
1 tbsp liquid honey
lemon juice to taste
2 blood oranges, peeled and sliced
1 small pineapple, peeled and diced
1 apple, cored and diced
2 bananas, peeled and sliced
2 tbsp coriander leaves

Blend the first three ingredients in a liquidiser. Toss the fruits and coriander in this dressing. Serve chilled.

BORN FOR BEER

(SERVES 4)

There has been great interest recently in different varieties of bottled beers. British breweries have, by and large, been very slow in reacting to customer demands and importing the different varieties needed to satisfy their constant lust for experimentation. Having said that, Hoegaarden, one of my favourites, a Belgian white beer, is imported by Whitbreads and is now widely available. This menu is good beer-drinking food with a Pickled Herring Salad and chicken in a Mexican green nutty sauce.

Pickled Herring Salad

1 jar (8-oz/225-g) wine-marinated herring, cut into 1-in (2.5-cm) pieces
1 hard-boiled egg, chopped
1 apple, cored and chopped
2 spring onions, sliced
2 sticks celery, finely sliced
½ pint (300 ml) soured cream

Combine all the ingredients, and serve with buttered rye bread.

Chicken in a Mexican Nutty Herb Sauce

4 tbsp peanut or corn oil
2 oz (50 g) flaked almonds
2 oz (50 g) peanuts, unsalted
2 oz (50 g) walnuts
5 medium-hot green chillies, diced
2 cloves garlic, chopped
4 greenish tomatoes, coarsely chopped
4 spring onions, sliced
1 bunch coriander, chopped
juice of 2 limes
1 pint (600 ml) chicken stock
1 x 3-lb (1.4-kg) smoked or cooked chicken, skin removed
salt and ground black pepper

Heat the oil and cook the nuts and chillies for approximately 3 minutes until the nuts are light brown, turning continuously. Transfer the nuts, chillies and oil to a food processor. Add the garlic, tomato, spring onion, coriander and lime juice, and blend to make a thick sauce. Pour the sauce, little by little, into the hot chicken stock until emulsified. Cut the chicken into 2-in (5-cm) chunks and add to the sauce. Heat through gently, not allowing it to boil.

Chilli-fried Potatoes

1 lb (450 g) new potatoes, thinly sliced
3 tbsp olive oil
1 tbsp chilli oil
1 chilli, finely diced
1 tbsp chopped coriander leaves
1 tbsp sliced spring onions
salt and ground black pepper

Pan-fry the new potatoes in the oils over a medium heat for 10 minutes, turning regularly. Toss with chilli, coriander leaves and spring onions and cook for a further 5 minutes, or until the potatoes are cooked and crispy. Season to taste.

LEARNING TO LIVE WITH LEFTOVERS

(SERVES 2)

I'm captain of a team on the Radio 4 foodie quiz, A Question of Taste. Often we have to produce a midnight snack from three bizarre ingredients: for instance, a mango, a tin of sardines and a parsnip. This poses no problem as I love producing dishes from any leftovers one might find in the fridge. Spontaneity and confidence are the name of the game. With leftovers in mind, this menu offers an eggy hash of asparagus, smoked bacon and spring onions, followed by roast lamb salad on a crispy potato cake.

Asparagus, Smoked Bacon and Spring Onion Hash

1 clove garlic, finely chopped
2 spring onions, sliced in 1-in (2.5-cm) pieces
2 oz (50 g) smoked bacon diced
1 tbsp olive oil
1 tsp capers
8 cooked asparagus spears, cut in 2-in (5-cm) pieces
1 tbsp diced black olives
1 tbsp balsamic vinegar
3 eggs
salt and ground black pepper

In a non-stick pan, fry the garlic, spring onions, and bacon in olive oil until golden. Add the capers, asparagus, olives and vinegar and heat through. Whisk the eggs and pour into the asparagus mixture. Stir until the eggs are cooked to your liking and resemble scrambled eggs. Season to taste and serve on hot buttered toast.

Roast Lamb Salad on a Potato Cake

3 medium potatoes, cooked and grated
1 onion, grated
2 tbsp chopped parsley
salt and ground black pepper
2oz (50 g) unsalted butter
1 egg yolk
1 tsp Dijon mustard
1 tsp finely chopped garlic
2 tsp lemon juice
2 tbsp soured cream
4 tbsp extra virgin olive oil
8 slices roast lamb
2 handfuls salad greens, such as rocket, baby spinach, little gem lettuce hearts, radicchio
3 tbsp soft herb leaves, such as chervil, flat parsley, tarragon, coriander, basil

Combine the potato, onion, parsley and seasoning, place in a 9-in (22-cm) non-stick frying pan and flatten into a thin potato cake. Cook in hot butter in a non-stick frying pan until golden, then flip over and repeat. In a bowl whisk together the egg yolk, mustard, garlic, lemon juice and soured cream. Add three-quarters of the oil slowly until emulsified; season. Cut the potato cake in two, and toss the lamb with the salad leaves, herbs and the remaining olive oil. Place on top of the potato cake and dribble with the creamy garlic dressing.

SEDUCING THE SEASONS

(SERVES 6)

I was challenged on Richard and Judy's This Morning programme to cook two dishes in the time it takes to reheat a TV supper from one of the supermarkets. This was live TV and, as with all these magazine programmes, your time invariably gets reduced. It was – I ended up with just over 5 minutes, but managed to cook both dishes with 5 seconds to spare, hair-raising stuff! I cooked a pasta dish and a squid and mediterranean vegetable casserole; do try this, it's excellent. Precede it with Last-of-the-Season Leek and First-of-the-Season Pea Soup.

Last-of-the-Season Leek and First-of-the-Season Pea Soup

2 leeks, washed and chopped
2 oz (50 g) unsalted butter
1 tsp soft thyme leaves
1 clove garlic, finely chopped
1½ pints (900 ml) chicken or vegetable stock
10 oz (275 g) shelled or frozen peas
1 round lettuce, washed and chopped
1 tbsp finely chopped mint leaves
½ pint (300 ml) double cream (optional)
salt and ground black pepper

Cook the leeks in the butter with the thyme and garlic until soft but not brown. Add the stock and bring to the boil. Add the peas and lettuce and continue cooking until the peas are tender. Stir in the mint leaves and, if you desire, the cream; liquidise. Return to the heat, season to taste and serve with a few croutons.

Mediterranean Squid and Vegetable Casserole

2 onions, roughly chopped
4 tbsp extra virgin olive oil
2 cloves garlic, chopped
2 anchovies, mashed
1 chilli, finely diced
8 oz (225 g) aubergine, peeled and cut
In 1-In (2.5-cm) cubes
2 tbsp oregano or marjoram leaves
2 tbsp ripped basil leaves
8 oz (225 g) courgettes, sliced
2 red peppers, roasted and then peeled
and seeded
4 tomatoes, skinned, seeded and quartered
1 tbsp balsamic vinegar
2 lb (900 g) squid, cleaned and cut in to
small squares
salt and ground black pepper

Cook the onion in half the olive oil with the garlic, anchovies and chilli until the onion is soft but not brown. Add the aubergine and cook for 5 minutes, turning regularly. Add the oregano, basil and courgettes and cook until the courgettes start to wilt. Finally, add the roast red peppers, tomatoes and vinegar. Heat through. Meanwhile, while the vegetable mixture is cooking, pan-fry the squid in the remaining olive oil over a high heat for about 1 minute: do not allow the squid to overcook otherwise it will become very tough. Just before serving, add the squid to the vegetables. Season to taste.

GRATEFULLY IRISH

(SERVES 4)

I often teach at Ballymaloe Cookery School near Cork in Southern Ireland. I always come away feeling that I could easily live there: beautiful countryside, beautiful people and wonderful ingredients. One of my latest restaurants, The Atrium in Millbank, Westminster, serves a great selection of all that's good about Ireland, and this menu produces an Irish offering of White Soda Rolls and a dish of Mussels with Bacon.

White Soda Bread or Rolls (Arán Sóide)

1 lb (450 g) white flour, preferably unbleached
1 level tsp salt
1 level tsp bicarbonate of soda
1 level tsp caster sugar
12 fl oz (350 ml) buttermilk

Preheat the oven to 230°C/450°F/Gas 8. Sieve the dry ingredients into a mixing bowl. Make a well in the centre and pour in most of the buttermilk. Using one hand in a circular motion, mix in the flour to form a dough which is softish without being too wet or sticky - add more buttermilk if necessary. Turn the dough out on to a floured board. Knead just enough to tidy the package into a neat ball. For bread, pat the dough into a round 1¼ in (3 cm) deep and cut a deep cross on the surface. Bake for 15 minutes on a floured baking tray then reduce the heat to 200°C/400°F/Gas 6 for another 30 minutes. To test whether cooked, tap the bottom of the bread and if it is ready it will sound hollow. For rolls, flatten the dough to 1 in (2.5 cm) deep and cut in 2-in (5-cm) circles. Bake for about 20 minutes at the higher temperature.

Mussels with Bacon (Diúlicíní Agus Bagún)

½ pint (300 ml) dry cider
5 lb (2.25 kg) small mussels, cleaned
8 slices streaky bacon, cut into thin strips
½ onion, finely diced
6 sage leaves, finely chopped
1 apple, peeled, cored and diced
salt and ground black pepper
2 oz (50 g) unsalted butter, chilled and diced

In a large saucepan, bring the cider to a fast boil, add the mussels and cover with a lid. Cook for 3-5 minutes, shaking the pan occasionally. Remove the mussels from their shells and keep warm. Strain the mussel liquor, return it to the heat and boil until reduced by half. Meanwhile, in a frying pan, cook the bacon with the onion and sage until the bacon is crisp. Add the apple and cook for a further 3 minutes. Season with salt and ground black pepper. Return the mussels to the boiling liquor and fold in the cold butter pieces. Divide the mussels and their liquor between four warm bowls. Scatter with the bacon mixture and serve with the warm bread or new potatoes and a leaf salad.

CHECKING OUT THE CHILLI
(SERVES 4)

Once upon a time a chilli was just a chilli; you never knew what strength to expect. You either blew your head off, or you wondered what all the fuss was about. It is quite the opposite in America where you are offered over one hundred varieties with exotic names such as Malagueta, Chawa, Chilaca and Poblano, ranging from 1 degree of heat to 10. Recently, enterprising suppliers have started our initiation process and some varieties can be found in supermarkets. This menu offers a simple Chicken, Chilli and Corn Soup followed by Grilled Mackerel with Chilli and Horseradish.

Chicken, Chilli and Corn Soup

4 jalapeño (medium-strength) chillies,
seeded and finely diced
2 slices streaky bacon, diced
1 onion, finely diced
1 clove garlic, finely diced
2 oz (50 g) unsalted butter
1 tsp soft thyme leaves
1 medium-sized potato, peeled and diced
2 chicken breasts, skinned and diced
8 oz (225 g) fresh, frozen or
canned corn niblets
2 pints (1.2 litres) chicken stock
¼ pint (150 ml) double cream

Pan-fry the chilli, bacon, onion and garlic in the butter until the onion is soft. Add the remaining ingredients, with the exception of the cream, and simmer, covered, for 20 minutes. Season to taste and finish with the double cream.

Grilled Mackerel with Chilli and Horseradish

4 x 12-oz (350-g) mackerel, very fresh
1 tsp diced hot chilli
salt and ground black pepper
⅓ pint (200 ml) good olive oil
2 spring onions, finely diced
2 tsps grated horseradish (not creamed)
½ tsp dried chilli flakes
1 tsp chopped rosemary leaves
juice of 1 lemon

Slash the mackerel two times on each side, place a little chilli in each cut and season with salt and black pepper; rub with a little of the olive oil. Place the fish under a hot grill or on a barbecue (weather permitting). Cook for approximately 7 minutes each side or until the skin is crispy and the fish is cooked through. Meanwhile, heat the remaining oil with the spring onions, horseradish, dried chilli and rosemary. Cook for 2 minutes and add lemon juice and salt to taste. Drizzle over the mackerel and serve with a leaf salad and new potatoes.

HAPPY TO BE HEALTHY

(SERVES 4)

After eating at the heaving Wagamama restaurant in London, one comes away feeling light in the stomach and heavy in the pocket – healthy food at rock-bottom prices. A few times a year I have this health craze which usually only lasts a couple of days, but it's the thought that counts. I start it off with some thinly sliced scallops and a green mango salad and then straight into a bowl of Soup Noodles.

Scallops with Green Mango

8 raw diver-caught scallops,
thinly sliced horizontally
2 tbsp liquid honey
2 tbsp nam pla (Thai fish sauce)
2 tbsp lime juice
2 green mangos, peeled and finely diced
(if unavailable use tart green apples)
2 tomatoes, seeded and finely diced
1 bunch spring onions, finely sliced
4 tbsp finely chopped coriander leaves
2 tbsp finely chopped lemongrass
1 tsp finely chopped garlic
1 tsp finely chopped red chilli
extra coriander leaves

Arrange the scallop slices on four chilled plates. Combine all the remaining ingredients and divide between the four plates. Garnish with coriander leaves and serve.

Soup Noodles

12 oz (350 g) udon or thin noodles
2 pints (1.2 litres) good chicken stock
3 fl oz (85 ml) soy sauce
4 tbsp dry sherry or mirin
(a Japanese sweet wine)
1 tbsp liquid honey
2 oz (50 g) shiitake mushrooms,
stems removed
1 leek, washed and finely sliced
2 oz (50 g) broccoli florets
2oz (50 g) Chinese cabbage, sliced
2oz (50 g) sugar snap peas
4 eggs
ground black pepper

Cook the noodles until *al dente* in boiling, salted water then drain. Meanwhile, bring the stock, soy sauce, mirin and honey to the boil; add the noodles. Arrange the vegetables on top and carefully break in the 4 eggs, keeping them separate. Cover and cook until the eggs are set. Season, pour into a large bowl and serve immediately.

EGGS FOR BREAKFAST
(SERVES 1)

Eggs have taken a bit of a hammering in the last couple of years, whether for too much cholesterol, or as a source of food poisoning in such things as mayonnaise or hollandaise. Things appear to be back to normal but, as far as I'm concerned, I rarely pay attention to food scares. If you like eggs, you eat them, and here's a delicious breakfast, extolling their virtues.

Sunday Morning Kick-start

1 tbsp caster sugar
1 egg
2 shots dark rum
1 shot brandy
¼ pint (150 ml) milk
grated nutmeg

Beat the sugar with the egg until pale and creamy. Heat the rum with the brandy and pour over the egg and mix well. Pour into a tumbler and top up with iced milk and ice cubes. Top with grated nutmeg. For cold winter days heat the milk and omit the ice cubes.

Egg on Egg Omelette

½ apple, peeled, cored and diced
2 oz (50 g) unsalted butter
3 eggs
salt and ground black pepper
1 hard-boiled egg, chopped
2 tbsp diced ripe Brie
2 tsp soured cream

Pan-fry the apple in half the butter until starting to soften. Set aside. Crack the eggs into a small bowl and beat together until combined. Season. Melt the remaining butter in an non-stick omelette pan until foaming but not coloured, then tip in the eggs. Keeping them moving with a fork, by drawing the edges to the centre. Fill the centre with apple, hard-boiled egg, cheese and soured cream. Fold the omelette over to the far lip of the pan and turn on to a plate. Serve with crispy fried tomatoes.

Crispy-fried Tomatoes

4 oz (100 g) plain flour
1 tsp garlic powder
½ tsp ground cumin
salt and ground black pepper
2 unripe tomatoes, cut into ½-in (1-cm) slices
1 egg beaten with ½ pint (150 ml) milk
unsalted butter

Combine the flour with the garlic powder, cumin, salt and ground black pepper. Dip the tomato slices in the flour mixture, then in the egg and finally one more time in the flour. Pan-fry in butter for about 3 minutes each side until golden brown.

A TOUCH OF SPICE

(SERVES 4)

One of the excellent cookbooks I recently read was Ismail Merchant's Passionate Meals. It has inspired me to resurrect my interest in Indian cookery, even if his approach tends to be slightly 'westernised'. I have adapted his spicy fish curry for the main course and added a salad made from tandoori chicken which can easily be purchased from major supermarkets.

Tandoori Chicken Salad

1½ lb (675 g) cooked tandoori chicken
½ lb (225 g) tomatoes, seeded and diced
1 bunch spring onions, sliced
2 green chillies, diced
2 tbsp chopped coriander
10 oz (275 g) Greek yogurt
2 tbsp chopped mint
2 tbsp lemon juice
½ tsp powdered cloves
salt and ground black pepper
salad leaves

Combine the first five ingredients in a bowl. In another bowl mix together the next four ingredients to make a dressing. Toss the chicken mixture in this dressing and season to taste. Serve on a bed of salad leaves.

Spicy Fish Curry

1½ lb (675 g) fish fillets,
such as salmon, cod or monkfish
vegetable oil
2 onions, thinly sliced
6 cloves garlic, finely diced
½ tsp ground coriander
¼ tsp turmeric
½ tsp cayenne pepper
½ tsp ground ginger
3 tomatoes, seeded and chopped
8 oz (225 g) leaf spinach, stems removed
½ tsp salt
5 oz (150 g) Greek yogurt
1 tsp liquid honey

Cut the fish into 1-in (2.5-cm) cubes and pan-fry in hot oil until lightly browned all over. Remove from the pan and set aside. Add a little more oil to the pan and fry the onion until soft but not brown. Add the garlic and spices and cook for a further 5 minutes. Combine the onion mixture with the tomato and spinach and cook until the spinach has wilted. Season with the salt, then add the yogurt and honey. Bring to the boil and simmer for 5 minutes. Return the fish to the sauce and heat through. Serve immediately with plain rice.

BREAKFAST MEETS LUNCH

(SERVES 2–4)

It's funny how food trends come and go. At the moment poached eggs are all the rage, which is great for you at home because the perfect poached egg is cooked ahead, kept in water in your fridge, and then reheated in boiling salted water just before consumption – perfect for pre-planned brunches. This menu offers Poached Eggs with Parma Ham and Mushrooms followed by a delicious brunch dish, Chopped Peppered Lamb Steak

Poached Eggs with Parma Ham and Mushrooms

2 oz (50 g) unsalted butter
8 oz (225 g) button mushrooms, sliced
½ tsp soft thyme leaves
¼ pint (150 ml) double cream
salt and ground black pepper
3 tbsp white wine vinegar
4 large free-range eggs
6 thin slices Parma ham

Heat the butter in a frying pan over a medium heat, then add the mushrooms and thyme and cook until the mushrooms release their juices. Increase the temperature and cook until the liquid has all but disappeared. Add the cream, cook until it has thickened, and season to taste. Meanwhile, fill a saucepan with enough water to cover the eggs, add the white wine vinegar and bring to the boil. Reduce the heat until you have a slow rolling boil, and break the eggs one at a time directly into the water. Cook until the whites are firm and the yolks runny. Arrange three slices of ham around the outside of each plate, place the mushrooms in the middle and top each with two poached eggs. (If you want to plan ahead, both the poached eggs and mushrooms can be prepared in advance and warmed through prior to serving.)

Chopped Peppered Lamb Steak

1 lb (450 g) minced lamb (20% fat)
crushed black peppercorns
12 cloves garlic
1 bay leaf
1 sprig thyme
½ pint (300 ml) water
olive oil
3 tbsp chopped mint
2 oz (50 g) unsalted butter,
cut in small cubes
salt and ground black pepper

Shape the lamb into four 'burgers' and coat them all over with crushed pepper. Poach the garlic, thyme and bay leaf in the water for about 15 minutes or until the garlic is tender. Remove the garlic and reserve; strain the liquor and keep for later. In a hot frying pan with a little oil, sear the burgers with the garlic cloves for 2 minutes on each side. Lower the heat and cook for a further minute each side, depending on how rare you like your meat. Remove the burgers and the browned garlic and keep warm. Pour the garlic liquor into the lamb pan (there should be about 4 fl oz/120 ml). Add the mint and butter and whisk to emulsify. Put the lamb and garlic on warm plates, season and top with the sauce. Serve with a leaf salad.

LUNCH ON A BUDGET

(SERVES 4)

Surely there are times when you get a craving for soft-boiled eggs with toasted 'soldiers', eggs Benedict or a creamy plate of scrambled eggs? Another dish I enjoy is a classic French number, hot Potato Salad with Mollet Eggs, and I follow this with Wine-pickled Mackerel, which should be prepared ahead. This mackerel dish represents excellent value as at present it's an unfashionable fish.

Potato Salad with Mollet Eggs

1½ lb (675 g) new potatoes, washed
6 large eggs
3 shallots, finely diced
5 tbsp good olive oil
salt and ground black pepper
1 tbsp sherry vinegar
½ bunch parsley, chopped

Cook the potatoes in salted water until tender, then drain and cut in half. Keep warm. Meanwhile lower the eggs into boiling salted water and cook for exactly 6 minutes: mollet eggs are not a variety of egg but a method of cooking where the whites are hard and the yolks are soft but not runny. Run the eggs under cold water and when cool enough to handle, remove the shells. Cut the eggs in half lengthways and arrange in a dish with the potatoes. In a frying pan cook the shallots with the olive oil until soft, sprinkle with salt and pepper, add the vinegar and parsley, and pour the entire contents over the eggs and potato.

Wine-pickled Mackerel

4 x 6-oz (175-g) mackerel fillets
1 tbsp olive oil
1 bottle dry white wine
1 tsp fennel seeds
4 cloves garlic, crushed
2 sprigs thyme
1 bay leaf
1 large onion, sliced
2 carrots, thinly sliced
1 tsp white peppercorns
2 sprigs parsley
1 stalk celery, sliced

Arrange the mackerel in a lightly oiled baking tray. In a non-reactive saucepan combine the remaining ingredients and over a moderate heat simmer for 15 minutes. Pour the contents of the pan over the mackerel and simmer for a further 8 minutes. Transfer the fish and cooking liquor to a earthenware or china dish, cool and refrigerate. Remove the bay leaf and parsley sprigs. Serve the next day, chilled, with sliced cucumber mixed with yogurt and some chopped dill.

PROUD TO BE BRITISH

(SERVES 4)

As a great supporter of the 'Back British Food Campaign', I'm appalled at this country's continuing 'foodie inferiority complex'. It's about time we believed in ourselves and were proud of what we produce. The French buy our lamb, our shellfish, our game and even our sandwiches, and their food standards aren't bad, so let's put an end to a British disease of knocking everything we stand for. This menu includes seasonal Kentish asparagus and strawberries and that perennial favourite, Scottish beef.

Asparagus with Soft-boiled Eggs and Burnt Butter

1 lb (450 g) asparagus, trimmed
salt
4 free-range eggs
4 oz (100 g) unsalted butter
juice of ½ lemon

Cook the asparagus in boiling salted water for 6-10 minutes, depending on thickness. Drain and keep warm. In the same water boil the eggs for 4 minutes. When ready to eat, melt the butter in a saucepan over a medium heat until frothing golden, with a distinctly nutty aroma. Pour in the lemon juice. Eat by dipping each spear into the burnt butter and then into the soft egg yolk.

Rare Beef Salad

1 lb (450 g) Scottish rump or sirloin of
beef in one piece
salt and ground black pepper
2 tbsp lime juice
2 tbsp nam pla (Thai fish sauce)
2 tsp liquid honey
4 spring onions, sliced
1 cucumber, peeled and sliced in 1-in
(2.5-cm) chunks
3 tomatoes, cut in wedges
3 tsp finely chopped mint
salad leaves

Season the beef with salt and ground black pepper. Grill or pan-fry for about 4 minutes on each side. Allow to rest for 5 minutes, then slice thinly across the grain. Meanwhile, in a saucepan, combine the lime juice, fish sauce and honey. Cook for 2 minutes over a medium heat, then add the remaining ingredients except the leaves. Fold in the beef and mix well. Taste and season. Serve on dressed salad leaves.

Strawberries with Rum

¾ pint (450 ml) soured cream
6 oz (175 g) soft brown sugar
1 flat tsp ground cinnamon
4 fl oz (120 ml) Myer's dark rum
2 punnets strawberries, hulled and halved

Beat together the soured cream, sugar, cinnamon and rum until smooth. Place a little of this mix in the bottom of four glasses. Divide the strawberries amongst the glasses and top with the remaining sauce.

EASTER FOR TWO
(SERVES 2)

So it's Easter Sunday and, if you're like me, you haven't prepared anything special for this soulful day. This is one of those rare occasions when turkey rears its ugly head. I wonder what it had in common with Jesus Christ; it's strange that we eat the beast to celebrate both his birth and his death. As this fatted fowl originated in America, it was probably one of their plots to purge wild creatures from ravaging their countryside. Anyway, it's here to stay, so this menu means a sprint to your Sunday supermarket to buy a breast. I offer you pan-fried turkey with poached eggs and tarragon mustard sauce followed by melted Mars Bar over your favourite ice cream.

Turkey with Poached Eggs and Tarragon Mustard Sauce

2 shallots, finely diced
4 tbsp dry white wine
¼ pint (150 ml) chicken stock
¼ pint (150 ml) double cream
2 tbsp Dijon mustard
3 tbsp chopped tarragon
salt and ground black pepper
6 eggs
4 tbsp fresh breadcrumbs
2 tbsp grated Parmesan
½ tsp cayenne pepper
2 tbsp olive oil
2 x 6-oz (175-g) turkey cutlets (approx.
½ in/1 cm thick)
4 tbsp plain flour
1oz (25 g) unsalted butter

In a small saucepan combine the shallots, dry white wine and chicken stock and bring to the boil. Reduce by half over a high heat. Add the cream and cook until slightly thickened. Whisk in half the mustard and two-thirds of the tarragon; season to taste. Meanwhile poach four of the eggs in the normal way. Combine the breadcrumbs, Parmesan, remaining tarragon and cayenne pepper in one bowl. In another bowl whisk together the remaining eggs, mustard and 1 teaspoon of the olive oil. Dip the turkey cutlets in seasoned flour, then into the egg mixture and then into the breadcrumbs, shaking off excess crumbs. Pan-fry the turkey in the remaining olive oil and butter for 3 minutes each side or until golden and cooked through. Serve with the poached eggs and the mustard sauce.

Melted Mars Bars over Ice Cream

2 Mars Bars, each cut into 6
3 tbsp double cream
your favourite ice cream

Melt the Mars Bars with the cream over a medium heat - do not boil. Pour this hot gorgeous goo over the ice cream and spend Easter Sunday in heaven.

THE ALTERNATIVE EASTER

(SERVES 4)

On Easter Sunday last year I was in the United States of America, where you often see restaurants featuring a 'raw bar' — what do you expect? Oysters, clams, scallops, etc. I came across one place that took the 'raw' a little bit further with a selection of tartares on their menu, including raw chicken, turkey or duck. Don't panic, I'm not going to subject you to raw poultry without further research, but raw is good so this menu includes a selection of tartares that can provide the perfect 'chill-down' after traditional hot cross buns and the classic Easter egg hunt.

Tuna Tartare Rolled in Soft Herbs

2 hard-boiled eggs, peeled
1 raw egg yolk
1 tsp Dijon mustard
2 tsp tarragon vinegar
3 tbsp extra virgin olive oil
1 lb (450 g) loin of tuna, very finely diced
salt and ground black pepper
5 tbsp chopped soft herbs such as tarragon, chives, chervil, parsley
soy and Tabasco sauce

Mash the hard-boiled eggs and combine with the raw egg yolk, mustard, vinegar and extra virgin olive oil. Combine the tuna with this mixture, then season to taste. Mould the mixture into four 'burgers', and roll each one in the soft herbs. Serve with a leaf salad. Have soy sauce and Tabasco available for those who have a death wish.

Tartare of 'Rose' Veal with Parmesan

¾ lb (350 g) British veal fillet, finely diced
3 oz (75 g) thinly sliced Parma ham, diced
3 oz (75 g) Parmesan, freshly grated
2 raw egg yolks
2 tbsp white truffle oil
½ tsp finely chopped oregano
1 clove garlic, finely chopped
1 tsp finely chopped chervil
pinch curry powder
salt and ground black pepper

Before I get mobbed with protests about veal, I should point out that British veal or 'rose' veal as the Government is calling it, is reared in a humane way and fed on a healthy dose of iron and roughage which counteracts the clinical anaemia prevalent in 'crated' veal. On with the method: pure simplicity. Combine all the ingredients, season to taste, and serve with toasted country bread.

'Tartare' of Celeriac Rémoulade

1 bulb celeriac, peeled
3 tbsp lemon juice
2 tbsp grain Dijon mustard
¼ pint (150 ml) thick mayonnaise
¼ pint (150 ml) soured cream
4 tbsp snipped chives
salt and ground black pepper
chicory leaves

Cut the celeriac into ⅛-in (3-mm) slices, then into thin strips. Cut each strip into small dice. Mix together the lemon juice, mustard, mayonnaise and soured cream. Fold in the celeriac and the chives. Season to taste, and serve on a bed of chicory leaves.

SPRING HAS SPRUNG
(SERVES 4)

There's nothing nicer than English asparagus: the flavour is much more developed than the more abundant Californian or Israeli varieties. Its season is short, but worth waiting for. For a pud, I've found a use for the severely criticised kiwi fruit. It took a bit of a hammering during our period of nouvelle cuisine madness, but it deserved it for it seemed to find its way on to every plate. This menu starts you off with a Salad of Asparagus with Avocado and Walnuts, followed by a Fruit Soup with Kiwi Juices.

Salad of Asparagus with Avocado and Walnuts

24 sticks English asparagus, trimmed
1 Haas avocado, peeled and sliced
4 tbsp lemon juice
4 tbsp light soy sauce
½ tbsp grated ginger
1 clove garlic, crushed with a little salt
12 fl oz (350 ml) extra virgin olive oil
4 tbsp boiling water
salt and ground black pepper
2 heads chicory
4 oz (100 g) lamb's lettuce washed
2 tbsp broken walnuts
2 tbsp snipped chives

Cook the asparagus in fast boiling water for 6 minutes, drain and refresh in iced water; drain again and set aside. Toss the avocado with half the lemon juice. For the dressing, combine the remaining lemon juice, soy, ginger, garlic and oil in a liquidiser or food processor for 30 seconds. Add the water and process for a further 30 seconds, then season to taste. Arrange six chicory leaves on each of four plates, dress the lamb's lettuce with some of the dressing and place in the centre of each plate. Scatter with the walnuts and the avocado. Dip the asparagus in the remaining dressing and place one stick on each of the chicory leaves. Scatter with the chives. Any remaining dressing will keep for a couple of weeks.

Fruit Salad with Kiwi Juices

½ pint (300 ml) Gewürztraminer wine
4 tbsp liquid honey
12 kiwi fruit, peeled
2 Granny Smith apples, peeled and cored
2 tbsp fresh lemon juice
1 mango, peeled, stoned and diced
10 large strawberries, hulled and halved
½ pineapple, peeled and cubed

Heat the wine and honey together, bring to the boil and then allow to cool to room temperature. In a food processor, blend eight of the kiwi fruit with the wine and honey mixture. Cut each remaining kiwi into eight wedges. Dice the apples and toss with the lemon juice. Combine all the fruit pieces in the centre of a bowl, ladle the kiwi juice around them, and chill until ready to eat.

MEMORIES OF WINTER

(SERVES 6)

We may have had some great weather recently, but I'm sure the winter chills are not over so, no, I'm not going to give you barbecue food yet. Instead a compromise: a light orientally-inspired dish of asparagus with oyster sauce followed by Schnuggies in a Skillet, a wonderfully comforting dish based on pan haggerty but with a few AWT add-ons. This dish may take a smidgen over 30 minutes but it is well worth the wait.

Oystered Asparagus

1½ lb (675 g) asparagus, trimmed
1 tsp cornflour
5 tbsp Chinese stock
2 tbsp Chinese oyster sauce
2 tbsp Katchup Manis (Indonesian sweet soy sauce) or soy sauce
1 tbsp sesame oil
1 tbsp vegetable oil
½ clove garlic, finely chopped
2-in (5-cm) knob fresh ginger, peeled and bruised
4 spring onions, sliced
1 tbsp liquid honey
salt and ground black pepper

Cut the asparagus on the diagonal into 1-in (2.5-cm) lengths. Blanch in boiling salted water for 30 seconds and plunge into iced water. Drain on paper towels and set aside. Mix together the cornflour, 1 tbsp warm stock (made from Chinese stock cubes, available in most supermarkets), the oyster sauce and Katchup Manis or soy. Heat the oils in a wok or frying pan over a high heat, then add the garlic, ginger and spring onions. Press down with the back of a ladle to release the aromatic juices. Add the asparagus and the remaining stock. Season with salt, pepper and honey. Cook the asparagus for 2 minutes, turning constantly. Pour in the oyster sauce mixture and bring to the boil. Remove the ginger, and toss the asparagus once again to coat evenly. Serve immediately.

Schnuggies in a Skillet

1 lb (450 g) onions, grated
3 oz (75 g) Cheddar cheese, grated
3 oz (75 g) Mozzarella cheese, grated
4 oz (100 g) streaky bacon, cut in strips
4 oz (100 g) chorizo sausage, cut in strips
1 tbsp mixed fennel seeds, rosemary and thyme leaves
2 cloves garlic, finely chopped
pinch nutmeg
salt and ground black pepper
2 tbsp olive oil
2 tbsp clarified butter
1 lb (450 g) potatoes, peeled and finely sliced
butter

Combine the onion, cheeses, meats, herbs, garlic, spice and seasonings. Set aside. Place a 9-in (23-cm) heavy skillet or shallow casserole over a medium heat and add the oil and clarified butter. Layer half the potatoes over the base, season and top with the onion mix. Cover with the remaining potato and then dot the top with softened butter. Cover with foil and cook on top of the cooker for 15 minutes. Remove the foil and cook for a further 15 minutes. Place the skillet under a hot grill to colour the top potato layer.

BREAKING FOR SUMMER

(SERVES 4)

Usually it's good weather in May, but make the most of it because, if the weather's anything like the past couple of years, May is Summer. It's a beautiful month, the countryside is vibrant and everyone is smiling as they shake off their winter blues. It's time to drink Pimm's, our only seasonal drink, and to start developing cold soups and fiery barbecues. This menu give you a Cold Pea Soup with Scallops, Mint and Sorrel, followed by Mussel Saté with Ginger and Coconut.

Cold Pea Soup with Scallops, Mint and Sorrel

6 spring onions, finely sliced
1 sprig thyme
1 tbsp vegetable oil
3 tbsp dry white wine
1 lb (450 g) shelled or frozen peas
½ lb (225 g) washed spinach, stalks removed
2 tsp caster sugar
salt and ground black pepper
4 scallops, shucked and cleaned
8 sorrel leaves, finely shredded
2 tbsp chopped mint leaves

Cook the spring onions and thyme in the vegetable oil over a medium heat for 5 minutes. Add the wine and 1½ pints (900 ml) water. Bring to the boil and add the peas; cook until the peas are tender, about 5-10 minutes depending on whether they are fresh or frozen. Add the spinach and sugar, cook for another minute and liquidise in a blender. Season to taste and allow to cool. Thinly slice the raw scallops and arrange them in the bottom of four soup bowls; scatter with sorrel and mint and a grinding of black pepper. Allow your guests to help themselves to the soup. The soup can be served hot.

Mussel Saté with Ginger and Coconut

24 green lip New Zealand mussels, defrosted
2 tbsp olive oil
spice mix of equal parts garlic powder,
ground black pepper, powdered white
pepper and cayenne pepper
2 oz (50 g) unsalted butter
4 shallots, finely sliced
2 tbsp finely chopped garlic
3 tbsp finely chopped ginger
2 chillies, finely chopped
¼ pint (150 ml) dry white wine
1 tbsp nam pla (Thai fish sauce)
1 tbsp ground white pepper
½ pint (300 ml) unsweetened coconut milk
1 tbsp liquid honey
½ pint (300 ml) double cream
2 tbsp chopped coriander

Thread three mussels on each of eight wooden skewers. Brush with a little of the olive oil and lightly dust with spice mix. Set aside. Melt the butter with the remaining olive oil over a medium heat. Add the shallots, garlic, ginger and chillies, and cook for 5 minutes without browning. Add the wine, fish sauce and white pepper and bring to the boil. Cook for a further 5 minutes. Add the coconut milk, honey and double cream and boil rapidly until liquid has reduced by half. Pass through a fine sieve. Add the coriander and keep warm. Chargrill or grill the mussel saté for 2 minutes each side. Serve immediately with the sauce, accompanied by a leaf salad and steamed rice.

NEW-SEASON FARE

(SERVES 2)

We are at that time of year when British products are starting to come into their own: wonderful new-season lamb, English asparagus, young broad beans, the tiniest of peas and the first of the Kent strawberries. Foods seem to taste so much better when eaten in their true seasons. The trouble now is that we buy so much from Kenya, California, the Antipodes and the rest of the world, we tend to forget the beauty of the seasons. The menu today is grilled goat's cheese on a salad of raw peas and broad beans followed by grilled lamb with asparagus and new potatoes.

A Salad of Goat's Cheese, Peas and Broad Beans

2 x Crottin or other variety of small
goat's cheese
salt and ground black pepper
1 bunch watercress, leaves only
1 tbsp picked tarragon leaves
1 tbsp picked flat parsley
2 spring onions, finely sliced
3 oz (75 g) shelled peas
3 oz (75 g) shelled broad beans, inner
skins removed
2 tbsp hazelnut or walnut oil
2 tbsp olive oil
1 tbsp lemon juice
1 tbsp grated Parmesan
2 tomatoes, chopped

Preheat the grill. Season the cheeses and cook under the grill until the top starts to melt, about 3–4 minutes. Meanwhile, combine the watercress and herbs with the spring onions, peas, broad beans, oils, lemon juice and Parmesan. Season to taste with salt and ground black pepper. Place the salad on two plates and top with the goat's cheese. Garnish with chopped tomatoes and serve with wodges of crusty bread.

New-season Lamb with Asparagus and New Potatoes

10 oz (275 g) Jersey Royal
potatoes, scrubbed
2 sprigs mint
4 oz (100 g) unsalted butter
1 tbsp finely chopped mint
1 tbsp finely chopped parsley
2 tbsp redcurrant jelly
1 tsp chopped rosemary
4 chump chops
1 tsp olive oil
8 oz (225 g) asparagus, trimmed
salt and ground black pepper

Place the new potatoes in salted water with the mint sprigs. Cook until tender, then drain and toss with half the butter, ground black pepper and the chopped mint and parsley. Meanwhile, melt the redcurrant jelly with 1 tbsp water and the rosemary. Brush the chops with oil and season with salt and ground black pepper. Grill for 3-4 minutes on each side, depending on how pink you like your lamb. When cooked, brush with the melted redcurrant jelly. Plunge the asparagus into fast-boiling salted water and cook for 6-10 minutes, depending on how thick it is. Drain and toss with the remaining butter. Season with ground black pepper. Serve the chops with the potatoes and the asparagus.

SUMMER MENUS

SPICE THE BIRD Caesar Salad
Spicy Chicken on the Run

TRENDY CARROTS Champagne Carrot Cappuccino
Escalopes of Pork with Sage Potato Crisps

SOUP AND A SANDWICH Bread and Tomato Soup
Hot Stuffed Croissant

STIRRING THE FIRE Spicy Avocado Dip
Shrimps from Hell

AN EVERYDAY LOBSTER The Lobster Club Sandwich
Stewed Plums in Spiced Rosemary Syrup

A RETURN TO CHILDHOOD Marmite Sandwiches
Cream Cheese and Sardine Sandwich
The Best Cucumber Sandwich

SAVOURY SNACKS Gremlins on Horseback
Chicken Kebab Tonnato

TOMATOES WITH TASTE Tomato and Basil Salad
Spaghetti with Classic Tomato Sauce

CHILLING OUT Champagne Punch
Avocado and Goat's Cheese Crostini
Asparagus with Prosciutto

LAST OF THE SUMMER SALADS Oriental Lobster Salad with Mint and Coriander
Warm Calf's Liver Salad with Balsamic Vinegar

SUNNY DAYS Guacamole Soup
The Caesar Salad Sandwich

ASIA MEETS FRANCE	Asian Chicken Salad
	Orange Nut Salad with Camembert
HEALTH IN THE SUN	Avocado with Tuna and Wasabi Sauce
	Button Mushrooms, Jumbo Shrimp and Spinach
	Raw Potato and Crab Salad
THE TRUE BRIT STRAWBERRY	The Strawberry Blonde
	Chilled Strawberry Zabaglione
	Strawberry Mascarpone
TABASCO MAGIC	Large Jug of Sangrita
	Traditional Spicy Chicken Wings
	with Blue Cheese Dip
A BRITISH SUMMER	Fresh Lemonade
	Baked Salmon and Cream with Dill and Cucumber
	Gooseberry and Elderflower Compote
THE OPENING BARBIE	Chargrilled Figs with Taleggio Cream
	Grilled Leg of Lamb with Chimichurri Sauce
DAIRY PLEASURES	Italian Chicken Soup
	Pan-fried Prawns in Gorgonzola Sauce
APOLOGIES TO BANGKOK	Thai-inspired 'Wardorf' Salad
	Seared Salmon with Wilted Spinach
	and Oriental Bits
SUMMER IN THE CITY	Raw Artichoke and Parmesan Salad
	Grilled Kidneys and Bacon on Mushroom
	Tapénade Toast
FEELING KIND OF SPANISH	Red Pepper Gazpacho with Frozen Olive Oil
	Smoked Chicken, Prawn, Chicory and Walnut Salad

IS IT BARBIE WEATHER?	Chargrilled Radicchio with Parmesan Shavings
	Chargrilled Calf's Liver with Balsamic Dressing
A SERIOUSLY SERIOUS BRUNCH	Perfect Bloody Mary
	Salmon Hash with Crispy Bacon and Avocado
OVERDOSING ON COURGETTES	Fettucine with Overcooked Courgettes
	Raw Courgette and Parmesan Salad
A SUMMER COLD	Cucumber Yogurt Soup
	Thai-inspired Melon Salad
INSPIRING NIGEL	Spiced Tomato Tart
	Souvlakia
FOR THOSE SELECTIVE MOMENTS	Stuffed Courgette Flowers
	Fettucine with Sea Urchins
COLD SOUP, HOT CHICKEN	Cold Pea and Mint Soup with a Broad Bean Salad
	Barbecued Gingered Chicken
MODERN TRAT	Bruschetta with White Bean Purée and Raw Mushrooms
	Tagliatelle with Butter and Rocket

SPICE THE BIRD

(SERVES 4)

'Spice is nice, but spice is difficult.' Why is there this perception that anything spicy takes brains or some uncanny chef's skills? It doesn't. Neither does it take long. However, I would advise that you marinate the chicken in this dish overnight — OK, so that takes a little longer than the half hour you're allowed, but in pure preparation terms it takes less than the required time. Now what are we going to start with? I suggest the classic Caesar Salad. Whether it is classic or not is for you to judge; the many so-called purists have different views. What the hell, it tastes good; that's all that matters.

Caesar Salad

2 oz (50 g) country bread, cubed
6 fl oz (175 ml) extra virgin olive oil
1 coddled egg (boiled for 1 minute)
juice of ½ lemon
1 tsp English mustard
½ tsp Worcestershire sauce
2 cloves garlic, chopped
1 x 2-oz (50-g) tin anchovy fillets, drained
ground black pepper
2 heads cos lettuce,
ripped into bite-sized pieces
2 oz (50 g) Parmesan, freshly grated

Preheat the oven to 150°C/300°F/Gas 2. Dribble the bread cubes with a little olive oil and place in the oven until golden and crisp, about 15 minutes. Allow to cool. In a food processor add the coddled egg (*sans* shell), the lemon juice, mustard, Worcestershire sauce, garlic and half of the anchovies. Blend until smooth. With the machine running, add the remaining olive oil in a steady stream until thickened. Season to taste with ground black pepper; salt is unnecessary on account of the anchovies. Toss the salad leaves with the dressing and the remaining anchovies, cut small. Add the Parmesan, toss again, and top with the croûtons.

Spicy Chicken on the Run

4 cloves garlic, crushed with salt
½ pint (300 ml) Greek yogurt
1 tbsp grated onion
1 chilli, finely diced
1 tsp each ground coriander, cumin,
fenugreek, paprika and ginger
pinch dry mustard
4 chicken breasts, cut in to strips

Mix together the garlic, yogurt, onion, chilli and spices. Add the chicken and marinate overnight (sorry). Wipe most of the yogurt from the chicken and chargrill or grill for 4 minutes on each side. Serve with rice or noodles and the strained marinade. Cold, the chicken makes a great filling for sandwiches.

A Salad of Goat's Cheese, Peas and Broad Beans

The Lobster Club Sandwich

Strawberry Mascarpone

Raw Artichoke and Parmesan Salad *(front)*; Raw Courgette and Parmesan Salad *(back)*

TRENDY CARROTS

(SERVES 4)

There was a time whenever you went to a dinner party you were offered carrot soup in one guise or other, quite often carrot and orange or carrot and coriander. On one of these jaunts I was offered carrot and champagne soup, brilliant and in vogue, as all the masters are knocking out cappuccino (frothy) soups and this effect is created by the last minute addition of champagne. To follow, Escalopes of Pork with Sage Potato Crisps.

Champagne Carrot Cappuccino

2 tbsp olive oil
4 oz (100 g) onions, finely chopped
1 tbsp crushed coriander seeds
12 oz (300 g) carrots, peeled and finely sliced
2 bay leaves
1 stick celery, finely sliced
6 oz (175 g) potatoes, peeled and finely diced
2 pints (1.2 litres) vegetable stock
1/2 pint (300 ml) Champagne or sparkling wine
salt and ground white pepper

In a heavy-bottomed saucepan, heat the olive oil over a medium heat. Add the onion and coriander seeds and cook for about 7 minutes. Add the carrots, bay leaves, celery and potato and cook for 1 minute. Pour in the vegetable stock and half the wine and bring to the boil. Simmer for about 15 minutes or until the vegetables are tender. Purée the soup in a food processor or liquidiser until smooth. Pass through a fine sieve. Check the seasoning. When ready to serve, reheat gently. Pour a couple of tablespoons of Champagne into each bowl when serving. The soup will fizz gently.

Escalopes of Pork with Sage Potato Crisps

8 x 3-oz (75-g) fillets of pork
olive oil
2 baking potatoes, peeled
24 sage leaves
3 oz (75 g) clarified unsalted butter or ghee
salt and ground black pepper
2 oz (50 g) hard unsalted butter
juice of ½ lemon
1 tsp chopped sage leaves
1 lemon, quartered

Preheat the oven to 180°C/350°F/Gas 4. Beat the fillets between sheets of clingfilm until you have ¼-in (5-mm) escalopes. Set aside until ready to cook. Line a baking sheet with greaseproof paper brushed with a little oil. Using a mandolin or electric slicer, cut the potatoes lengthways paper thin (do not rinse), keeping the slices in order as you are going to rebuild the potato. Place two adjacent slices of potato together with a sage leaf sandwiched in between. Assemble the remaining slices in the same way, and brush on both sides with clarified butter. Arrange them on the greaseproof paper and bake in the oven for 15 minutes or until golden. Set aside and keep warm. When ready to serve, heat 2 tbsp of the olive oil in a frying pan over a high heat. Season the escalopes and pan-fry them for 2 minutes each side; set aside and keep warm. Add the hard butter in pieces to the same pan and, when frothing, add the lemon juice and the chopped sage. Pour over the pork and serve with the crisps and a wedge of lemon.

SOUP AND A SANDWICH

(SERVES 4)

There are times when all I fancy is a quick bowl of soup and a sandwich. Never be fooled by all you hear of chef's eating habits, as quite often I'll just open a can of Heinz tomato soup, or a can of their baked beans. To this delicious canned tomato soup I would add a knob of butter and a dollop of double cream; perfect comfort food for a cold day. But this is not for inspired cooks at home. The following menu is equally comforting, starting with a thick Bread and Tomato Soup, backed up with a hot croissant stuffed with melting Brie over watercress and sliced pears. A perfect way to top up your energy-giving carbohydrates.

Bread and Tomato Soup

4 fl oz (120 ml) extra virgin olive oil
3 cloves garlic, finely diced
6 anchovy fillets, finely chopped
1 onion, finely diced
2 x 15-oz (425-g) cans chopped tomatoes
with basil
1 pint (600 ml) vegetable stock or still
mineral water
8 oz (225 g) olive oil bread,
crusts removed
½ bunch basil, leaves only
salt and ground black pepper

Heat half of the extra virgin olive oil in a large saucepan and add the garlic, anchovies and onion. Cook until soft but not brown, then add the tomatoes and stock or mineral water. Bring to the boil over a high heat and cook for 20 minutes, stirring from time to time. Break the bread into small chunks and fold into the soup. Combine until the bread has softened and is well mixed with the tomatoes. Add the basil leaves and season to taste with a little salt and plenty of ground black pepper. Finish the soup with a dribble of the remaining olive oil.

Hot Stuffed Croissant

4 buttery croissants
1 bunch watercress
2 pears, peeled and cored
8 oz (225g) ripe Brie
salt and ground black pepper

Preheat the oven to 200°C/400°F/Gas 6. Slice the croissants horizontally in two. Pick the watercress into small florets and arrange on the bottom half of the croissants. Slice each pear in half and then each half into six slices. Divide these slices between the four croissants. Top the pears with slices of Brie. If you wish, you can cut off the Brie crust, but this isn't necessary. Season with a little salt and ground black pepper. Top with the croissant lid and pop into the preheated oven and heat through until the Brie is meltingly gooey and soft.

STIRRING THE FIRE

(SERVES 2)

Chillies always excite my taste-buds. This menu includes a couple of fiery dishes that can be used to tease the gastric juices. To start, Spicy Avocado Dip, akin to a guacamole, served with crostini or corn chips, then a great shrimp dish packed full of flavour.

Spicy Avocado Dip

1 ripe avocado, peeled and stoned
1 tomato, seeded and diced
2 spring onions, sliced
juice of 1 lime
1 chilli, finely chopped
pinch ground cumin
pinch ground coriander
2 tbsp finely chopped coriander
1 tsp chilli oil
salt and ground black pepper

Mash the avocado with the back of a fork; do not make it too smooth. Fold in all the other ingredients and season to taste. Serve with crostini or corn chips.

Shrimps from Hell

3 fl oz (85 ml) vegetable oil
4 dried red chillies
2 cinnamon sticks, broken
6 cardamom pods, crushed
4 cloves
1 tsp chopped fresh ginger
1 tsp finely chopped garlic
6 bay leaves
1 lb (450 g) raw jumbo shrimps,
shells on
3 fresh green chillies, sliced
1 tsp turmeric
2 tsp ground cumin
1 tsp salt
¼ pint (150 ml) dry Martini

Heat the oil over a medium flame. When hot, stir in the dried chillies, cinnamon, cardamom, cloves, ginger, garlic and bay leaves. Cook for 4 minutes, then increase the heat and add the shrimps. Cook for 3 minutes, turning from time to time, then remove the prawns and keep warm. To the same pan add the green chillies, turmeric, cumin, salt and dry Martini. Cook for a further 5 minutes, stirring regularly. Return the prawns to the pan and warm through. Serve immediately with a large salad and a bowl of steamed rice.

AN EVERYDAY LOBSTER
(SERVES 2)

Oh, that lobster was an everyday food. The 'cheap' season for this élite food is summer, so take the opportunity to splash out on a crazy idea, the lobster club sandwich, 4 in (10 cm) thick and worth every penny. At the other end of the financial scale, pick yourself some plums and enjoy a forgotten pud of stewed plums in a spiced rosemary syrup.

The Lobster Club Sandwich

6 slices streaky bacon
2 tbsp olive oil
6 slices country bread
½ pint (300 ml) good mayonnaise
1 head Belgian chicory, broken into bite-sized pieces
2 x 1-lb (450-g) cooked lobsters, meat removed
juice of ½ lemon
2 hard-boiled eggs, sliced
salt and ground black pepper
18 slices cucumber
2 plum tomatoes, sliced

Cook the bacon in a frying pan until crispy; set aside. To the bacon fat add the olive oil and, in the combination of hot fats, fry four slices of bread on one side only until golden. Lay the four fried slices (crispy-side down) and two fresh slices of bread on the work surface. Spread the uncooked sides with mayonnaise. Top two of the fried slices with chicory, followed by lobster, lemon juice, more mayo and the sliced egg; season. Top this combo with the uncooked bread, then cucumber, bacon and tomato; season. Top with the remaining slices fried-face up. Secure each sandwich with two cocktail sticks and slice in half. Serve with *frites* or crisps.

Stewed Plums in Spiced Rosemary Syrup

¼ pint red wine
6 oz (175 g) caster sugar
1 sprig rosemary
1 bay leaf
1 strip each lemon and orange rind
2 cloves
2-in (5-cm) cinnamon stick
6 blacks peppercorns, crushed
1 lb (450 g) plums, washed

Bring the first eight ingredients to the boil and simmer until the sugar has dissolved. Add the plums and cover with a lid. Cook gently until the plums are soft but still whole. Remove the plums and set aside. Strain the juices and return to the heat. Boil until thick and syrupy. Pour over the plums and serve hot or cold with thick cream.

A RETURN TO CHILDHOOD

(SERVES 6)

The various shows, including the BBC Good Food Show, where I'm invited to demonstrate provide me with the perfect platform for my 30-minute menu. In anticipation of the stress this causes me, I often eat simply and revert back to childhood sandwich favourites made on unfashionable sliced bread.

Marmite Sandwiches

Take Marmite and three times as much butter and mix to a paste. Spread liberally on slices of bread. Place slices of bread together and cut into shapes to suit your fancy. Chopped cress, grated carrot or thinly sliced cucumber can be added for variety.

Cream Cheese and Sardine Sandwich

1 x 250-g pack Philadelphia cream cheese
2 x 120-g cans sardines in oil
3 tsp creamed horseradish
1 tsp lemon juice
ground black pepper

Mash all the ingredients together and season with a good quantity of black pepper. A little salt may be required. Spread this mixture on to thinly sliced buttered bread. Top with cucumber slices if required.

The Best Cucumber Sandwich

1 cucumber, peeled and thinly sliced
1 small pack Philadelphia cream cheese
juice squeezed from 2 tbsp grated onion
2 tbsp mayonnaise
salt and ground black pepper

Soak the cucumber slices in salted water for up to half an hour. Drain, dry and chop; add to the Philadelphia cheese softened with a little onion juice and some mayonnaise. Season to taste.

SAVOURY SNACKS

(SERVES 2)

Snacking is a necessity for those who have a frantic schedule. Usually it's grab a sandwich and eat on the run. However, for those times when you have a little more time, but you still only fancy a couple of mouthfuls rather than a full-blown meal, how about Gremlins on Horseback, a cheeky interpretation of the angels made with soft herring roes, and mini chicken kebabs with tuna sauce?

Gremlins on Horseback

6 soft herring roes
6 slices streaky bacon
juice of ½ lemon
salt and ground black pepper
4 oz (100 g) unsalted butter
3 slices bread, crusts removed
Patum Peperium or anchovy paste
1 tbsp chopped thyme leaves
½ red onion, diced

Wrap each roe in bacon, securing with a cocktail stick. Sprinkle with lemon juice and a little salt. Fry gently in half of the hot butter for 3 minutes on each side until the bacon is slightly crispy. Remove from the pan and keep warm. Add the remaining butter to the pan, slice the bread in two diagonally and fry both sides until golden. Spread the bread with Patum Peperium or anchovy paste. Top each triangle of bread with the gremlin and scatter with thyme, red onion and black pepper.

Chicken Kebab Tonnato

½ onion, finely diced
½ carrot, finely diced
½ stick celery, finely diced
2 cloves garlic, finely diced
½ tsp soft thyme leaves
1 bay leaf
2 tbsp olive oil
1 x 200-g can tuna in oil
4 canned anchovy fillets
½ pint (300 ml) dry white wine
¼ pint (150 ml) mayonnaise
1 x 8-oz (225-g) chicken breast, skinned and cut into ½-in (1-cm) dice
salt and ground black pepper

Cook the onion, carrot, celery, garlic, thyme and bay leaf in the oil until the onion is soft but not brown. Add the tuna, anchovy and white wine and simmer for 20 minutes or until ⅙ pint (3½ fl oz (100 ml) liquid remains. Remove the bay leaf and blend in a food processor until smooth. Allow to cool, then fold in the mayonnaise. When ready to eat, thread the chicken on to four satay or cocktail sticks and grill for 3 minutes on each side. Season with salt and black pepper. Serve the hot kebabs with the cold tuna sauce.

TOMATOES WITH TASTE
(SERVES 2)

This is the time of year when tomatoes have some taste. Too often tomatoes are hot-house grown, with perfect shape and perfect colour, but are tasteless. What I want are sun-kissed tomatoes, which may not always have the perfect shape — maybe a few skin blemishes — but are jammed full of flavour. Let's start off with a simple Tomato and Basil Salad with tomato crostini, then a steaming bowl of spaghetti with a classic tomato sauce. You can make the sauce in bulk and freeze or preserve it.

Tomato and Basil Salad

3 tbsp extra virgin olive oil
6 diagonal ¼-in (5-mm) slices French baguette
1 clove garlic, halved
6 large, ripe, firm tomatoes
6 canned anchovy fillets
½ bunch basil, leaves only
1 tsp balsamic vinegar
1 tbsp diced red onion
Maldon salt and ground black pepper
rocket leaves

Preheat the oven to 180°C/350°F/Gas 4. Dribble about 1 tbsp of the olive oil over the baguette slices and cook in the oven until golden and crispy. Remove from the oven and allow to cool. Rub the surface of each crostini with a piece of garlic clove. Slice the tomatoes and place three slices on each crostini. Top each crostini with a fillet of anchovy and a basil leaf. Dress the remaining slices of tomato with the remaining olive oil and the balsamic vinegar. Rip the remaining basil leaves, then top the tomato slices with red onion, basil, Maldon salt flakes and ground black pepper. Serve the tomato salad with rocket leaves and tomato crostini.

Spaghetti with Classic Tomato Sauce

½ onion, finely diced
2 cloves garlic, finely diced
1 stick celery, finely diced
4 tbsp virgin olive oil
1 lb (450 g) tomatoes, peeled and quartered
1 tbsp caster sugar
¼ pint (150 ml) red wine
3 tbsp ripped basil leaves
1 tbsp chopped parsley
8 oz (225 g) dried spaghetti
salt and ground black pepper

Cook the onion, garlic and celery in the olive oil until soft but not brown. Add the tomatoes, sugar and red wine. Cook for 20 minutes over a medium heat, stirring from time to time. (For a pizza topping, cook for 40 minutes.) Remove from the heat and fold in the basil and parsley. Meanwhile, in abundant, fast-boiling, salted water cook the spaghetti until tender but still with a little bite; drain. Toss the spaghetti with the sauce, season to taste and top with the Parmesan.

CHILLING OUT

(SERVES 6)

A light summery lunch is always welcome. When it's hot, nobody wants to bother with the preparation of an elaborate lunch. Just knock up a quick snack that can be eaten in the garden. A jug of Champagne punch, some crostini topped with avocado and goat's cheese, then a plate of Asparagus with Prosciutto. Crostini bases can be made in advance and kept crispy in a sealed plastic container.

Champagne Punch

2 bottles Chablis, chilled
2 pineapples, peeled, cored and sliced
4 white sugar lumps
2 tbsp lemon juice
2 tbsp brandy
2 bottles Champagne

Combine the first five ingredients and allow to marinate as long as possible. Add the Champagne just before consuming.

Avocado and Goat's Cheese Crostini

18 thin slices baguette
1 clove garlic, halved
extra virgin olive oil
1 ripe avocado, peeled and diced
4 oz (100 g) soft goat's cheese
1 tbsp lemon juice
1 tbsp chopped basil
1 tbsp diced red onion
salt and ground black pepper

Preheat the oven to 180°C/350°F/Gas 4. Brush the bread slices with the garlic and a little olive oil. Bake in the oven until golden and crispy; about 10 minutes. Allow to cool. Meanwhile, mash the avocado with the goat's cheese. Fold in 2 tbsp olive oil, the lemon juice, basil and onion. Season to taste. Top each crostini with a mound of the avocado mixture.

Asparagus with Prosciutto

1½ lb (675 g) fresh asparagus, woody stems removed
4 tbsp extra virgin olive oil
1 tbsp balsamic vinegar
2 tbsp snipped chives
salt and ground black pepper
1 lb (450 g) thinly sliced prosciutto

Plunge the asparagus into plenty of boiling salted water and cook for approximately 8 minutes, or until it is tender with just a little crunch. Drain and keep warm. Combine the olive oil with the balsamic vinegar, chives and seasoning. Toss the warm asparagus in the dressing while still warm. Allow to cool. Serve with the prosciutto.

LAST OF THE SUMMER SALADS

(SERVES 4)

Each year I wait in anticipation for the start of our Indian summer, and get most upset when it passes us by. If temperatures take a turn for the better I enjoy the 'Last of the summer salads', two touches of luxury: Oriental Lobster Salad with Mint and Coriander and a warm Calf's Liver Salad with Balsamic Vinegar.

Oriental Lobster Salad with Mint and Coriander

juice of 2 lemons, grated rind of 1
3 spring onions, sliced
2 tbsp nam pla (Thai fish sauce)
1 tbsp caster sugar
2 red chillies, seeded and cut in thin strips
meat from 3 x 1-lb (450-g) cooked lobsters
2 tbsp chopped mint leaves
2 tbsp chopped coriander leaves
4 oz (100 g) sugar snap peas, topped and tailed

Combine the first five ingredients and stir until the sugar has dissolved. Cut the lobster flesh into bite-sized pieces and add to the dressing with the mint and coriander. While the lobster is marinating, blanch the sugar snaps in plenty of boiling salted water for 2 minutes. Drain the peas and plunge into icy water to arrest the cooking and set the colour. Just before serving, toss the lobster with the peas. Check seasoning.

Warm Calf's Liver Salad with Balsamic Vinegar

6 oz (175 g) baby spinach leaves
2 oz (50 g) unsalted butter
1 tbsp olive oil
4 shallots, cut in quarters
1 tsp soft thyme leaves
4 x ¼-in (5-mm) slices pancetta or streaky bacon, cut into strips
1 lb (450 g) calf's or lamb's liver, cut in nuggets
24 clean button mushrooms
12 black olives
salt and ground black pepper
2 tbsp pine nuts
1 tbsp balsamic vinegar

Wash and dry the baby spinach leaves and arrange on four plates. Heat the butter and olive oil in a frying pan and fry the shallots until brown and softening. Add the thyme, pancetta and liver and increase the heat; cook the liver until brown but still pink in the middle. Remove liver, shallots and pancetta and keep warm. In the same pan, fry the mushrooms and olives for about 5 minutes. Return the liver mixture to the pan and toss together, then season. With a slotted spoon, place an equal amount on each plate. Add the pine nuts to the butter remaining in the pan and cook until golden. Deglaze the pan with the vinegar and spoon a little of the warm dressing over each salad.

SUNNY DAYS

(SERVES 4)

I look forward every year to our meagre ration of British sun; in recent years rationing has gone by the board and we've been given a full diet of sun, sun, sun. Talking of diet, hot weather is not conducive to 'pigging out', so I should be as thin as a rake. I'm not, perhaps due to the fact that I eat too much guacamole soup and usually follow it with a chunky American caesar salad sandwich.

Guacamole Soup

2 large ripe avocados, peeled and diced
1 garlic clove, finely diced
3 tbsp lime juice
1 chilli, finely diced
½ tsp ground cumin
½ tsp ground coriander
½ pint (300 ml) + 6 tbsp double cream
1½ pints (900 ml) vegetable or chicken stock, chilled
salt and ground black pepper
2 tomatoes, seeded and diced
2 spring onions, finely sliced
2 tbsp finely chopped coriander
deep-fried tortilla strips

Combine the avocado, garlic, 2 tbsp of the lime juice, chilli, cumin, ground coriander, ½ pint (300 ml) double cream and the stock in a blender, and pureé until smooth. Season to taste. Ladle the soup into chilled bowls and garnish with tomatoes, spring onions, chopped coriander and the tortilla strips. Whip the remaining cream and lime juice to soft peaks and float a little of this on the surface of the soup.

The Caesar Salad Sandwich

2 cloves garlic, crushed with a little salt
2 tbsp chopped canned anchovies
1 tbsp grated lemon zest
1 oz (25 g) grated Parmesan
½ pint (300 ml) mayonnaise
4 large whole-grain brown rolls, cut in half, or 8 slices whole-grain brown bread
½ cos lettuce, ripped into bite-sized pieces
6 hard-boiled eggs, peeled and sliced
fresh Parmesan shavings

Fold the garlic, anchovies, lemon zest and grated Parmesan into the mayonnaise. Spread each side of the rolls/bread with this mayonnaise. Toss the cos lettuce with the remainder. Divide the egg between four halves, top with lettuce and finally the Parmesan shavings which are created by drawing a potato peeler over a chunk of fresh Parmesan. Season with plenty of black pepper and assemble the sandwich by topping with the remaining bread. Cut each sandwich in half and, as they say in America, enjoy.

ASIA MEETS FRANCE

(SERVES 6)

During the heat that Britain can experience, the last place I want to be is stuck in a sweaty kitchen or restaurant. I need to get outside to enjoy the sun (British or otherwise), so picnic fare is the order of the day: an oriental chicken salad followed by a melting Camembert with a fruit and nut salad.

Asian Chicken Salad

2 tbsp vegetable oil
2 tsp finely chopped garlic
1 tbsp finely chopped chilli
¼ pint (150 ml) fresh lime juice
2 tbsp nam pla (Thai fish sauce) or light soy sauce
2 tbsp liquid honey
3 cooked chicken breasts, shredded
2 green papayas, peeled and cut into matchsticks
3 tbsp chopped mint
3 tbsp chopped coriander
1 bunch spring onion, sliced
½ celeriac, peeled and cut into matchsticks
2 oz (50 g) unsalted peanuts, roughly chopped
salt and ground black pepper

Combine the first six ingredients and blend in a food processor until smooth. Mix the remaining ingredients with enough of the dressing to coat. Season to taste.

Orange Nut Salad with Camembert

1 head Belgian chicory, finely sliced
2 oz (50 g) broken walnuts
2 oz (50 g) slivered almonds, toasted
2 oranges, peeled and sliced
8 oz (225 g) seedless grapes
¼ pint (150 ml) fresh orange juice
3 tbsp fresh lime juice
2 tbsp liquid honey
½ tsp ground cinnamon
3 tbsp walnut oil
3 tbsp chopped mint
3 tbsp chopped dates
1 ripe Camembert

Combine all the ingredients for the salad and serve with wedges of the very ripe Camembert.

HEALTH IN THE SUN

(SERVES 4)

I always marvel when I achieve the impossible, a British 'tan'. I know it's not environmentally correct to sport a tan, but what would life be without the opportunity to break the rules from time to time? With the blazing sun, what better than some healthy, light Japanese salads which will, however, mean a trip to your local oriental hostelry.

Avocado with Tuna and Wasabi Sauce

2 tsp wasabi powder
3 tsp water
3 tbsp light soy sauce
4 oz (100 g) line-caught fresh tuna, cut in ½-in (1-cm) dice
2 avocados, peeled, and cut in ½-in (1-cm) dice
3 spring onions, finely sliced

Mix the wasabi powder with the water and leave to rest for 10 minutes. Fold in the soy sauce and combine with the tuna and avocado. Sprinkle the spring onion on top. (Use salmon if you can't buy fresh tuna.)

Button Mushrooms, Jumbo Shrimp and Spinach

6 oz (150 g) clean button mushrooms, sliced
12 cooked jumbo shrimps, peeled and sliced
3 oz (75 g) baby spinach, washed and dried
2 tbsp rice vinegar
2 tbsp lemon juice
1 tbsp light soy sauce
2 tbsp vegetable oil
3 spring onions, sliced

Mix together the mushrooms, shrimps and spinach. In a separate bowl combine the rice vinegar, lemon juice, soy sauce and vegetable oil. Pour this over the salad and sprinkle with the spring onions.

Raw Potato and Crab Salad

8 oz (225 g) new potatoes, peeled
1 tsp salt
4 tbsp mirin (a Japanese sweet wine)
4 tbsp rice vinegar
dash soy sauce
4 oz (100 g) fresh white crabmeat
1 sheet nori seaweed (optional), finely shredded

Cut the potatoes into julienne or fine matchsticks, sprinkle with half the salt and rest for 15 minutes. Meanwhile, combine the mirin, rice vinegar, soy sauce and remaining salt; bring to the boil over a medium heat. Allow to cool. Wash and dry the potatoes, then toss them with the crab and dressing. Sprinkle nori over the top, if desired. If the thought of raw potato does not appeal, use celeriac or carrot.

THE TRUE BRIT SRAWBERRY

(SERVES 4)

The Wimbledon tennis weeks are here again. The organisers must be looking nervously at the weather, as are the strawberry growers. Will there be enough home-grown or will the caterers have to resort to the imported varieties? Eat British where possible, they're so much tastier. To get you into the Wimbledon spirit, this menu is dedicated totally to strawberries .including a floater inspired by the beautiful Rita Hayworth in the film The Strawberry Blonde.

The Strawberry Blonde

1lb (450 g) strawberries, hulled
6 oz (175 g) caster sugar
¼ pint (150 ml) water
1 bottle Laurent Perrier Rosé Champagne
8 scoops Haagen-Dazs vanilla ice cream.

Liquidise the first three ingredients. Pass the purée through a fine sieve. In each ice cream soda glass or tumbler, combine ¼ pint (150 ml) Champagne with 4 tablespoons strawberry purée. Float a couple of scoops of ice cream on top.

Chilled Strawberry Zabaglione

2 punnets strawberries, hulled and sliced
4 tbsp caster sugar
4 egg yolks
6 tbsp strawberry purée (see above)
¼ pint (150 ml) double cream

Toss the strawberries in half the sugar. Beat the yolks and remaining sugar in a bowl set over a pan of simmering water. When the sugar dissolves add the strawberry purée and continue to beat until thick and frothy. Place the bowl over ice and continue to whisk until cool. Beat the cream to stiff peaks and fold into the zabaglione. Finally fold in the strawberries. Serve immediately.

Strawberry Mascarpone

2 punnets strawberries, halved
4 tbsp Strega or Amaretto
3 tbsp caster sugar
1 egg white
4 oz (100 g) Mascarpone cheese

Toss the strawberries with the liqueur and half the sugar. Whip the egg white to soft peaks, add the remaining sugar and continue beating to medium peaks. Fold in a little of the egg white into the Mascarpone, and stir until smooth. Fold in the remaining egg white. Divide the fruit amongst four bowls with their juices. Top with the Mascarpone.

TABASCO MAGIC

(SERVES 4)

On a trip to New Orleans I was given the opportunity to discover the secret of Tabasco sauce, now in its 127th year. What a great set up; a rare piece of foodie culture in a country where food history tends to be a little limited. What impressed me was its purity; no heat treatment, just the original recipe. Look out for an excellent Tabasco, green in colour, made with jalapeño chillies due in the UK soon. A couple of Tabasco-inspired recipes follow: a drink with a kick, followed by spicy chicken wings with a blue cheese dip.

Large Jug of Sangrita

1 small onion, diced
½ pint (300 ml) fresh orange juice
2 pints (1.2 litres) tomato juice
juice of 4 limes
1 tsp Worcestershire sauce
1 tsp caster sugar
1 tsp Tabasco sauce
Gold Tequila

Combine the first seven ingredients in a liquidiser and purée until smooth. Pour a large shot of tequila over ice and top up with the cocktail.

Traditional Spicy Chicken Wings with Blue Cheese Dip

¼ pint (150 ml) soured cream
¼ pint (150 ml) mayonnaise
2 tsp white wine vinegar
2 tbsp sliced spring onions
1 clove garlic, finely diced
2 tsp Tabasco sauce
3 oz (75 g) blue cheese, crumbled
salt and ground black pepper
vegetable oil for frying
12 chicken wings, cut in two
4 oz (100 g) unsalted butter, melted
1 tbsp Heinz tomato ketchup
cayenne pepper and salt

In a food processor blend together the soured cream, mayonnaise, vinegar, spring onions, garlic, half the Tabasco and the cheese. Season to taste and set aside. Heat about 2 in (5 cm) vegetable oil in a heavy saucepan to 180°C/350°F. Fry the wings, a few at a time, for about 6 minutes or until golden and thoroughly cooked. Drain on kitchen paper. Mix together the butter, ketchup and remaining Tabasco, toss the wings in this mixture and dust with cayenne pepper and salt. Serve hot with the blue cheese dip.

A BRITISH SUMMER

(SERVES 6)

For those 'blazing hot British days', what better than a refreshing cup of tea, to cool the parts that alcohol can't? No, well then, how about a jug of Fresh Lemonade – nothing better. I'm also giving you an old English salmon recipe and then a gooseberry compote infused with the flavour of elderflowers, found freely growing in lanes in the country. It will take a little longer than the prescribed 30 minutes but, if you allow it to cool, it makes a terrific 'fool' when mixed with lightly whipped cream.

Fresh Lemonade

juice of 12 lemons
grated rind of 6 of the lemons
6 oz (175 g) caster sugar
water or soda water

Mix the lemon juice with the lemon rind and the caster sugar until the sugar has dissolved. (Use less sugar if you prefer.) Chill and, when ready to drink, pour over ice cubes and add the same amount of water or soda.

Baked Salmon and Cream with Dill and Cucumber

3 oz (75 g) unsalted butter
4 spring onions, sliced
1½ lb (675 g) middle-cut salmon fillet
½ pint (300 ml) double cream
¼ pint (150 ml) water
1 cucumber, peeled, seeded, and diced
1 tsp grated lemon rind
½ bunch dill, chopped
salt and ground black pepper

Preheat the oven to 400°F/200°C/Gas 6. Butter an ovenproof dish and scatter with the spring onions. Spread the remaining butter over the seasoned salmon. Mix the cream and water and pour around the salmon. Cover with foil and bake in the oven for about 15 minutes or until cooked to your liking. When cooked, remove the salmon and keep warm. Strain the cooking juices into another saucepan and bring to the boil. Cook until the sauce has reduced to the thickness of single cream. Add the cucumber, lemon rind and dill; season to taste. Pour over the salmon and serve with buttered new potatoes.

Gooseberry and Elderflower Compote

4 oz (100 g) caster sugar
½ pint (300 ml) water
1½ lb (675 g) gooseberries, topped
and tailed
5 heads elderflowers, tied with a thread
of cotton

Melt the sugar in the water by heating over a medium flame. Add the gooseberries and elderflowers. Simmer for about 15 minutes or until the gooseberries are cooked. Remove and discard the elderflowers. Eat the gooseberries hot or cold with cream or ice cream. For a 'fool', fold in ¼ pint (150 ml) lightly whipped cream or a mixture of cream and custard.

THE OPENING BARBIE

(SERVES 4)

It's time to extend your barbecuing techniques, summer demands it! No, that doesn't mean standing out in the freezing cold cooking great slabs of meat. Good barbies mean good marinating, and you can practise these techniques just as well indoors using a normal grill or oven. My menu begins with chargrilled figs wrapped in pancetta, a delicious combination served with Taleggio cream, followed by Grilled Leg of Lamb with Chimichurri Sauce. The lamb can be marinated in this sauce overnight for a more powerful flavour.

Chargrilled Figs with Taleggio Cream

6 figs, sliced in two
12 slices pancetta, or streaky bacon
4 sprigs thyme
1 tbsp extra virgin olive oil
salt and ground black pepper
1oz (25 g) unsalted butter
¼ pint (150 ml) double cream
5 oz (150 g) Italian Taleggio cheese, cut into cubes
1-2 tomatoes, sliced

Wrap each fig half in a slice of pancetta, enclosing some thyme leaves and a dribble of olive oil. Season with ground black pepper. Set aside while you make the sauce. Melt the butter, add the cream and Taleggio; simmer gently until all has combined and the cheese has melted. Season to taste. Whilst the sauce is cooking, grill or chargrill the figs until the pancetta is crispy. Serve the figs with the sauce and some tomato slices.

Grilled Leg of Lamb with Chimichurri Sauce

1 x 4-lb (1.8-kg) leg of lamb
3 cloves garlic, sliced

Sauce
1 pint (600 ml) cold water
¼ pint (150 ml) good olive oil
6 tbsp fresh oregano
8 cloves garlic, finely chopped
1 tbsp paprika
1 tbsp salt
1 tsp dried crushed red pepper
1 tsp ground black pepper
1 tsp ground white pepper

Ask your butcher to remove the central bone and 'butterfly' the leg of lamb. Make several incisions all over the meat and insert slices of garlic. Whisk together all the sauce ingredients, pour over the lamb and, if possible, leave overnight. Turn from time to time. If the overnight option doesn't come within your 30-minute schedule, bring the ingredients to the boil and baste the lamb whilst it is grilling. Chargrill the lamb to your desired requirements: 12 minutes each side should produce a medium-rare result. Serve with baby spinach salad, some chargrilled vegetables and a little sauce.

DAIRY PLEASURES

(SERVES 2)

My doctor advised me to forego one of life's greatest pleasures. No, not that; she suggested I cut cheese out of my diet. I'm not sure whether it was to do with my weight problem or whether it was doing my head in, but I almost stopped. I really miss having a nibble of Parmesan or lunching on a chunk of Cheddar. Occasionally the temptation is too much, so I'll knock up a bowl of chicken soup with eggs and Parmesan, followed by some Pan-fried Prawns in Gorgonzola Sauce with a bowl of pasta. Delicious – I feel like a pig in heaven.

Italian Chicken Soup

1 pint (600 ml) good chicken stock
1 glass red wine
2 eggs
2 tbsp freshly grated Parmesan
2 tbsp chopped parsley
1 tbsp snipped chives
good pinch grated nutmeg
salt and ground black pepper

Bring the stock to the boil; add the red wine. In a bowl beat together the eggs, Parmesan, parsley, chives and a good pinch of nutmeg. Pour this mixture into the hot broth in a continuous stream, stirring with a fork. Cook undisturbed for a further minute until the eggs are set. It will have a raggedy look but don't worry, it tastes delicious. Remember, looks aren't everything. Season to taste.

Pan-fried Prawns in Gorgonzola Sauce

8 oz (225 g) fresh fettucine
1 tbsp olive oil
salt and ground black pepper
16 large uncooked prawns, peeled
seasoned flour for dredging
1 oz (25 g) unsalted butter
2 tbsp dry Martini
1 tsp soft thyme leaves
¼ pint (150 ml) double cream
2 oz (50 g) Gorgonzola cheese, crumbled
1 oz (25 g) Parmesan, grated
2 tsp snipped chives

Cook the pasta in boiling salted water, then drain and toss with olive oil and ground black pepper. Keep warm. Dust the prawns with seasoned flour and fry them in hot butter for 2 minutes. Remove and keep warm. Deglaze the pan with the Martini, then add the thyme, cream, Gorgonzola and Parmesan and boil until the sauce slightly thickens. Return the prawns to the sauce. Season and add chives. Serve with the pasta.

APOLOGIES TO BANGKOK

(SERVES 2)

My mind often wanders off to happy days spent at the Oriental in Bangkok. Not that the following recipes have anything to do with the food at the Oriental, but they do have oriental influences. I start with a refreshing, mouth-tingling salad based on a classic Waldorf, followed with one of our 'cheapest' fish, salmon, liberally spiced with Szechuan peppercorns in an alcoholic sauce.

Thai-inspired 'Waldorf' Salad

1 apple, cored and diced
½ cucumber, peeled, seeded and diced
3 spring onions, sliced
6 radishes, sliced
1 tbsp broken macadamia nuts
1 tbsp chopped coriander
1 tbsp grated ginger
2 tbsp fresh lime juice
1 tsp liquid honey
1 clove garlic, finely diced
1 tbsp olive oil
2 tsp sesame oil
½ tsp chilli oil
1 head chicory, ripped into small pieces
salt

Combine all the ingredients, except the chicory and salt, in a large, non-reactive bowl. Season with salt. Refrigerate until the natural juices have been released. Just before serving, fold in the chicory. More chilli oil can be added if you feel in a 'blow your head off' mood.

Seared Salmon with Wilted Spinach and Oriental Bits

3 tsp Szechuan peppercorns, crushed
¼ pint (150 ml) saké
½ onion, finely diced
3 in (7.5 cm) fresh ginger, finely diced
1 chilli, finely chopped
3 tbsp rice vinegar
¼ pint (150 ml) double cream
2 x 6-oz (175-g) salmon fillets, skin removed
2 tbsp sesame oil
12 oz (350 g) spinach, stems removed
salt
2 tsp chopped coriander
2 tsp chopped spring onions

In a small saucepan over a medium heat combine 1 tsp of the peppercorns, the saké, onion, ginger, chilli and vinegar. Bring to the boil and cook for 6 minutes. Add the cream and simmer until the liquid thickens. Strain and keep warm. Meanwhile, dust the salmon fillets with the remaining crushed peppercorns. Heat the sesame oil in a frying pan until hot and cook the salmon for 1 minute each side (longer if you can't face raw interiors); remove and keep warm. Add the spinach to the same pan, and keep turning it over with tongs until it wilts. Season the sauce, salmon and spinach with salt. Place the spinach on two plates, surround with sauce and top with the salmon. Garnish with the coriander and spring onions.

SUMMER IN THE CITY
(SERVES 2)

No room for chat in this menu, but two delicious recipes none the less, with inspiration from the Med. Raw artichokes sound risky but are a revelation with the Parmesan and lemon, followed by bits and bobs on toast. I love toast: the Italians would call it bruschetta, but they probably wouldn't go along with the kidneys – very British country house.

Raw Artichoke and Parmesan Salad

2 large or 4 baby artichokes
2 fl oz (50 ml) extra virgin olive oil
1 tbsp freshly squeezed lemon juice
1 egg yolk
1 canned anchovy fillet, mashed
2 tbsp freshly grated Parmesan
grated zest of ½ lemon
salt and ground black pepper
6 basil leaves, ripped

Remove all the coarse outer leaves from the artichokes, especially if using large ones; cut off the tips and remove the hairy choke. Coarsely grate or very thinly slice the artichokes into a non-reactive bowl. Toss the gratings with the olive oil and lemon juice, then fold in the egg yolk, anchovy, Parmesan and lemon zest. Season to taste with a little salt and plenty of ground black pepper. Scatter with basil leaves.

Grilled Kidneys and Bacon on Mushroom Tapénade Toast

extra virgin olive oil
2 large field mushrooms, thinly sliced
1 clove garlic, crushed with a little salt
1 tsp fresh thyme leaves
3 fl oz (75 ml) red wine
3 tbsp chopped parsley and basil
2 tsp Dijon mustard
3 canned anchovy fillets, drained
2 tsp capers
12 black olives, pitted
salt and ground black pepper
6 lamb's kidneys, cut in half and trimmed
4 rashers streaky bacon
2 slices country bread

Heat 2 tbsp of the olive oil in a frying pan over a medium heat, add the mushrooms, garlic and thyme; cook, covered, for 5 minutes. Remove the lid, increase the heat and add the wine. Cook for a further 5 minutes or until most of the liquid has disappeared. Place the mushrooms in a food processor with the parsley, basil, Dijon mustard, anchovies, capers and olives, and process until roughly chopped and combined. With the machine still running, add 2 tbsp olive oil and season with black pepper. Meanwhile, throw the kidneys and bacon under a preheated grill. Cook for 2 minutes on each side, depending on how rare or crispy you like the kidneys and bacon. Toast the bread, dribble with olive oil and spread with some of the mushroom tapénade. Top with the bacon and kidneys. Season to taste.

FEELING KIND OF SPANISH

(SERVES 6)

A sunny lunch serving two cold dishes, both of which can be prepared ahead. To start, a cold soup based on the Spanish gazpacho, using red peppers in place of tomatoes. If you have the time and inclination, roast your own peppers until black, then skin, seed and use as stated in the recipe. The salad is a delicious summery combination; the smokiness of the chicken combines well with the walnuts and, for a touch of luxury, I've added a few peeled Mediterranean prawns. The Spanish usually float ice cubes on the top of the soup but I've suggested an AWT oddity – frozen olive oil.

Red Pepper Gazpacho with Frozen Olive Oil

2 slices white country bread
1 tbsp sherry vinegar
1 clove garlic, finely chopped
2 tsp caster sugar
1 red chilli, seeded
2 fl oz (50 ml) extra virgin olive oil
15 fl oz (450 ml) V8 juice
4 spring onions, sliced
1 x 425-g can red peppers, drained and roughly chopped
½ large cucumber, peeled and roughly diced
2 tsp pesto
salt and ground black pepper
8 cubes frozen extra virgin olive oil
8 basil leaves, ripped

Remove the crusts from the bread and break the slices into large crumbs. Place the bread in a food processor or blender. With the machine running, add the vinegar, garlic, sugar and chilli, and blend until smooth. Add the extra virgin olive oil. Then, a little at a time, add the V8 juice, spring onions, red peppers, cucumber and pesto. Continue to blend to form a smoothish emulsion. Season to taste with salt and black pepper. Pour into a bowl and garnish, just before serving, with frozen olive oil and ripped basil leaves.

Smoked Chicken, Prawn, Chicory and Walnut Salad

12 oz (350 g) peeled Mediterranean prawns
12 oz (350 g) smoked chicken meat
4 heads chicory
3 oz (75 g) broken walnuts
4 spring onions, sliced
1 apple, cored and diced
salt and ground black pepper
5 oz (150 g) Greek yogurt
3 tbsp lemon juice
3 fl oz (85 ml) walnut oil)
2 plum tomatoes, seeded and diced
1 tsp snipped chives

Cut the prawns, chicken and chicory into ½-in (1-cm) pieces. Combine well with the walnuts, spring onions and apple; season. In a separate bowl, mix together the yogurt and lemon juice. Slowly beat in the walnut oil as for mayonnaise, a few drops at a time. Just before serving, toss the salad ingredients with the dressing and mound on four plates. Garnish with diced tomatoes and chives.

IS IT BARBIE WEATHER?

(SERVES 2)

Another menu for the under-used barbie. We Brits have to learn to make snap decisions as, more often than not, the sun takes its hat off for no more than a couple of hours at a time. So this menu is a quick Italianate number starting with Chargrilled Radicchio with Parmesan Shavings, followed by thick slices of calf's liver with a balsamic dressing and some grilled vegetables.

Chargrilled Radicchio with Parmesan Shavings

¼ pint (150 ml) extra virgin olive oil
2 tbsp aged sherry vinegar
2 cloves garlic, crushed with a little salt
10 turns of fresh black pepper
1 large head radicchio, quartered
2 oz (50 g) Parmesan, in the piece
1 lemon, halved

Prepare the barbecue, allowing the coals to burn down. Combine the oil, vinegar, garlic and black pepper in a bowl. Allow the radicchio to marinate in this mixture for 5 minutes. Drain, then grill the radicchio for 2 minutes on each side. Using a potato peeler, shave the Parmesan into thin strips. Serve the radicchio on salad plates with the halved lemon and a scattering of Parmesan shavings.

Chargrilled Calf's Liver with Balsamic Dressing

3 fl oz (85 ml) balsamic vinegar
2 tbsp extra virgin olive oil
2 sprigs rosemary
2 tsp soft green peppercorns
1 shallot, finely diced
salt and ground black pepper
1 courgette, cut in 4 lengthways
1 small aubergine, cut in 4 lengthways
2 firm plum tomatoes, cut
horizontally in 2
2 x 5 oz (125 g) slices calf's liver
basil leaves

In a saucepan, mix together the first five ingredients. Season to taste and place on the side of the barbecue to heat through. Dip the vegetables in the marinade and grill for about 3 minutes on each side. This can be done at the same time as the radicchio and kept warm. Season the two slices of liver and brush with the balsamic dressing. Chargrill for between 4 and 8 minutes, depending on how rare you enjoy your liver, turning once. Serve and eat immediately with the grilled vegetables, a little of the balsamic dressing and a few ripped basil leaves.

A SERIOUSLY SERIOUS BRUNCH

(SERVES 4)

A quick brunch for the morning after the night before – I am persuaded to reveal the secret of 190 Queen's Gate's famous Bloody Mary. The base mix could be made the previous day, allowing flavours to develop overnight. This accompanies a salmon hash made simply with best-quality tinned salmon (it's the one with USA stamped on the lid), although fresh-cooked salmon could be used if tinned offends your natural juices. Crispy bacon and avocado salad provide contrasting textures. Finish off with strawberries in balsamic vinegar. Sounds yucky? Well, try it – you're in for a big surprise.

A Perfect Bloody Mary

2 fl oz (50 ml) Worcestershire sauce
1 tbsp Heinz tomato ketchup
1 tsp Tabasco sauce
1 tsp celery salt
5 tbsp freshly squeezed lemon juice
1 tbsp orange juice
1 tsp grated horseradish
(not creamed)
1 tsp finely chopped shallot or onion
½ tsp ground black pepper
3 pints (1.75 litres) V8 juice or tomato juice
2 tbsp dry sherry
ice cubes
vodka
4 celery sticks

Blend all the ingredients except the vodka and celery in a liquidiser. Transfer to a jug. Take ice-filled glasses, add slugs of vodka, top up with tomato mix and garnish with celery.

Salmon Hash with Crispy Bacon and Avocado

1 small red onion, finely diced
1 red pepper, seeded and finely diced
2 medium waxy potatoes, peeled and finely diced
3 tbsp olive oil
8 oz (225 g) canned Alaska salmon, drained
2 tbsp dill, finely chopped
salt and ground black pepper
4 eggs, lightly beaten
8 rashers bacon
2 avocadoes
2 tsp lemon juice
about 2 fl oz (50 ml) crème fraîche

In a non-stick frying pan, cook the onion, red pepper and potato in olive oil until tender and slightly brown (about 12 minutes). Transfer to a mixing bowl. Flake in the salmon and dill, season to taste; allow to cool for a few minutes. Add the eggs to the bowl and combine well. In a non-stick frying pan, heat the remaining olive oil. Spoon in the mixture to cover the whole pan. Allow to cook for approximately 5 minutes, then turn and brown the other side. Meanwhile, grill the bacon rashers until crisp; skin and mash the avocadoes with the lemon juice. To serve, cut the hash into wedges. Put dollops of crème fraîche at the side, along with a helping of the avocado and the crispy bacon.

OVERDOSING ON COURGETTES

(SERVES 4)

Nowadays we take courgettes for granted, but it's not so long ago that they were a luxury vegetable. Everybody tends to serve them very crunchy or al dente which is great, but they produce a wonderful pasta dish when cooked a little longer with extra virgin olive oil. To contrast, I serve a side salad of raw courgettes in a dressing akin to a Caesar. So the menu comprises Fettucine with Overcooked Courgettes and Raw Courgette and Parmesan Salad.

Fettucine with Overcooked Courgettes

4 fl oz (120 ml) extra virgin olive oil
1 onion, finely diced
2 cloves garlic, finely chopped
12 oz (350 g) courgettes, topped,
tailed and diced
1 tsp soft thyme leaves
1 tbsp chopped black olives
1 oz (25 g) unsalted butter
salt and ground black pepper
1 lb (450 g) fresh fettucine
2 oz (50 g) Parmesan, freshly grated

Heat the oil in a heavy-bottomed frying pan. Add the onion and cook over a medium heat until soft but not brown. Add the garlic, courgette and thyme; cook for a further 15 minutes, stirring gently from time to time. Add the black olives and the butter and stir to combine. Season to taste. Just before serving, cook the fettucine in plenty of boiling salted water until *al dente*, about 2-3 minutes depending on the freshness of the pasta. Drain and combine with the courgette sauce. Top the pasta with the grated Parmesan.

Raw Courgette and Parmesan Salad

12 oz (350 g) raw courgettes, grated
2 egg yolks
1 oz (25-g) canned anchovies,
finely chopped
1 clove garlic, finely chopped
1 tsp English mustard
juice of ½ lemon
4 fl oz (120 ml) extra virgin olive oil
ground black pepper
2 oz (50 g) Parmesan, freshly grated
6 basil leaves, shredded

Place the grated courgette in a large mixing bowl. In a food processor, blend the egg yolks with the anchovies, garlic, mustard and lemon juice. With the machine running, add the olive oil in a thin stream. Season to taste with black pepper; you don't need salt on account of the anchovies. Toss the courgette with enough of the dressing to coat liberally. Fold in the grated Parmesan and scatter the top of the salad with the basil leaves.

A SUMMER COLD

(SERVES 6)

Summer should be hot — here's hoping. For those blazing days we need to eat something refreshing, and what I ate in Thailand was a delicious melon salad with all sorts of melding flavours which will entail a trip to your oriental grocer; well worth the effort. To start, I suggest a light Cucumber Yogurt Soup. To drink, you name it, but a jug of sangria or Pimms seem to find the spot on hot sunny days.

Cucumber Yogurt Soup

3 large cucumbers, peeled and seeded
2 tsp salt
¼ tsp white pepper
3 cloves garlic, puréed with a little olive oil
1½ tsp ground cumin
1½ pints (900 ml) plain yogurt
1 bunch spring onions, thinly sliced
2 tsp chopped mint leaves

Roughly chop two of the cucumbers and finely dice the other. Purée the roughly chopped cucumber with the salt, pepper, garlic, cumin and yogurt. Strain through a sieve. Fold in the diced cucumber, spring onions and mint. Check seasoning and chill until ready to serve.

Thai-inspired Melon Salad

2 cloves garlic, puréed with a little olive oil
2 tbsp liquid honey or palm sugar
4 tbsp nam pla (Thai fish sauce)
4 tbsp lime juice
2 red chillies, finely diced
1 tbsp grated lime zest
2 oz (50 g) dried shrimp, finely chopped
2 oz (50 g) unsalted roasted peanuts
12 oz (350 g) water melon, peeled and chopped into 1-in (2.5-cm) dice
2 Galia or Ogen melons, peeled and chopped into 1-in (2.5-cm) dice
4 tbsp chopped coriander leaves
1 tbsp chopped mint leaves

In a large bowl, combine the garlic paste, honey, nam pla, lime juice, chilli and lime zest. Fold in the shrimp and peanuts. Add the two melons and stir to combine. Garnish with chopped coriander and mint. Chill until ready to serve.

Grilled Kidneys and Bacon on Mushroom Tapénade Toast

Salmon Hash with Crispy Bacon and Avocado

Butter-crumbed Eggs on Sorrel

Pan-fried Red Mullet with Tomatoes and Herbs

INSPIRING NIGEL

(SERVES 2)

I'm a great admirer of Nigel Slater who I think is destined to become one of Britain's great food writers. He has some wonderful ideas – lip-smacking, but easy on the pocket. For this menu I've nicked two of his dishes, one seemingly original and the other a classic. I start off with a Spiced Tomato Tart followed by the classic Greek Souvlakia.

Spiced Tomato Tart

6 oz (175 g) frozen puff pastry, defrosted
2 oz (50 g) unsalted butter
½ tsp ground coriander
½ tsp fennel seeds
3 spring onions, sliced
1 tsp ground cumin
2 cloves garlic, sliced
½ tsp chilli powder
5 tomatoes, thickly sliced
chopped coriander leaves

Preheat oven and a baking tray to 220°C/425°F/Gas 7. Roll the pastry out to ¼ in (5 mm) thick, and cut out either two rectangles or two circles. Prick the pastry shapes with the prongs of a fork. Allow to rest. In a frying pan, warm the butter over a medium heat. Add the ground coriander, fennel seeds, spring onions, cumin and garlic; stir-fry until the spices start releasing their fragrant bouquet. Add the chilli powder and the tomatoes, cook for 3 minutes then, with a slotted spoon, transfer the tomatoes to the top of the pastry, leaving a ⅓-in (1-cm) edge to the pastry. Transfer the tarts to the hot baking tray and cook in the oven for 15-20 minutes, until the pastry is risen and golden. Dribble a few of the tomato spice juices over the tart and serve with the coriander.

Souvlakia

8 oz (225 g) lamb fillets,
cut into ½-in (1-cm) slices
½ onion, grated
3 cloves garlic, mashed with a little salt
1 tsp ground black pepper
1 tsp ground cumin
½ tsp cayenne pepper
4 tbsp olive oil
2 pitta breads
juice of ½ lemon
4 tbsp Greek yogurt
½ tsp chopped mint leaves
½ tsp chopped coriander leaves
3 spring onions, sliced

Toss the lamb with the onion, garlic, black pepper, cumin, cayenne and olive oil. Allow to marinate for as long as possible but, if you're sticking to the 30-minute rule, 20 minutes will do. Heat a heavy-bottomed frying pan or griddle over a fierce heat. Cook the lamb in the pan, or alternatively chargrill or grill, for 2 minutes each side. Warm the pitta breads and cut the edges to form a pocket. Stuff the lamb into the pocket and dribble with lemon juice, yogurt, fresh herbs and the spring onion. Great snacking food.

FOR THOSE SELECTIVE MOMENTS

(SERVES 2)

If you have a patch of unused ground surrounding your house, then you must grow courgettes, not so much for the vegetable, more for the flower. These flowers can cost up to £1 each for we impoverished restaurateurs lusting after the delicate import, so grow them yourselves but use them as soon as you pick them. In this menu I'm going to stuff them, but they are equally as nice just dipped in batter and served with a herby tomato sauce. Then to be all-Italian, I'm going to blow you away with Fettucine with Sea Urchins. I admit sea urchins are not that readily available unless you live in Ireland or the Med, but bottled can be purchased ... a great dish if you can find them.

Stuffed Courgette Flowers

3 oz (75 g) plain flour
1 egg, beaten
½ tsp salt
4 tbsp milk
4 courgette flowers
3 oz (75 g) Mozzarella cheese, grated
1 tbsp grated Parmesan
1 tbsp chopped capers
1 tsp chopped sun-dried tomato
1 tbsp chopped basil
½ tsp tomato purée
salt and ground black pepper
vegetable oil for frying

Beat the flour, egg and salt together to create a paste. Add the milk to make a smooth batter. Set aside to rest. Remove the stamen from each flower. Mix together the stuffing ingredients except the oil and fill the inside of each flower with a little of the mixture. Heat the oil in a heavy saucepan, to a depth of 2 in (5 cm). Dip the flower into the batter, shaking off the excess. Fry the flowers until golden, turning once. This should take about 5-7 minutes. Drain on kitchen paper and serve immediately. This is an excellent dish with a green or red salsa.

Fettucine with Sea Urchins

14 fresh sea urchins
4 tbsp extra virgin olive oil
1 clove garlic, crushed with a little salt
1 shallot, finely diced
¼ pint (150 ml) white Burgundy
½ pint (300 ml) fish stock
salt and ground black pepper
10 oz (250 g) fresh fettucine
3 tbsp chopped flat parsley leaves

Open the sea urchins by inserting the point of a pair of scissors into the flatter side of the shell and cutting a circle to reveal five yellow or orange tongues (strips). Remove these and discard the shell. Heat the olive oil in a heavy frying pan, add the garlic and shallot; cook until the shallot is soft. Add the sea urchin flesh and the wine and cook until the liquid has all but evaporated. Add the fish stock and reduce by half. Season to taste. Cook the pasta in plenty of boiling salted water until *al dente*, about 3-4 minutes depending on the freshness of the pasta. Drain and add to the sauce. Toss with the parsley to combine.

COLD SOUP, HOT CHICKEN

(SERVES 4)

Some cold soups are wonderful for summer, but if you take the cool-down factor, they take a little longer than 30 minutes. You could of course be ultra trendy and technical and own a blast chiller...no?...then how about stirring the soup over ice. Better, just forget about the 30 minutes and allow me to instruct you on the beauties of cold pea and mint soup with a raw broad bean salad, followed by barbecued ginger chicken breasts.

Cold Pea and Mint Soup with a Broad Bean Salad

1½ pints (900 ml) vegetable stock
1 clove garlic, crushed with a little salt
4 spring onions, sliced
1 tbsp vegetable oil
1 lb (450 g) shelled fresh peas (frozen if necessary)
1 tbsp caster sugar
2 tbsp chopped mint leaves
salt and ground white pepper
½ pint (300 ml) single cream
6 oz (150 g) shelled and skinned broad beans
3 tbsp extra virgin olive oil
1 tsp lemon juice
3 tbsp grated Parmesan

Heat the vegetable stock. In another saucepan cook the garlic and spring onions in the vegetable oil until the onion is soft but not brown. Add the peas and sugar and pour over the boiling stock. Cook for 12 minutes if you are using fresh peas, 4 minutes if frozen. In a liquidiser, blend the soup with the mint. Season to taste and cool. When sufficiently chilled, add the cream. Just before serving combine the broad beans with the olive oil and lemon juice. Season with salt and plenty of ground black pepper. Fold in the Parmesan. Make a small pile of the salad in the centre of four soup plates, pour the soup around and serve immediately.

Barbecued Gingered Chicken

2 in (5 cm) fresh ginger, grated
½ onion, grated
1 chilli, finely diced
2 cloves garlic, crushed with a little salt
1 tbsp soy sauce
2 tbsp vegetable oil
2 tbsp liquid honey
4 chicken breasts, skin on
fresh coriander leaves

Combine the ginger, onion, chilli, garlic, soy, oil and honey and spread this mixture over the chicken. Leave to marinate for as long as possible. Heat the barbecue or grill. Cook the chicken for 7 minutes each side, basting with the marinade juices from time to time. Scatter the chicken with coriander leaves and serve with a simple leaf salad.

MODERN TRAT
(SERVES 4)

Fashions come and go, none more so than food. Gone are the days when one used to see the same dishes on the majority of restaurant menus, week after week, month after month, year after year. The one restaurant culture that survives all fashion is Italian. OK, so bruschetta has made an entry and rocket too, but they are there on merit. This menu gives you a simple modern Italian Bruschetta with White Bean Purée and Raw Mushrooms, followed by Tagliatelle with Butter and Rocket.

Bruschetta with White Bean Purée and Raw Mushrooms

extra virgin olive oil
4 garlic cloves, 3 finely diced
2 tsp finely chopped rosemary leaves
1 x 420-g can of cannellini beans, drained
¼ pint (150 ml) cold vegetable stock
salt and ground black pepper
4 oz (100 g) button mushrooms, sliced
juice of ½ lemon
1 tbsp chopped oregano leaves
4 thick slices country bread

In a saucepan, combine 3 fl oz (85 ml) of olive oil, the diced garlic and the rosemary; cook over a gentle heat until the garlic is soft but without colour. Add the beans, stir to combine, then cook for about 10 minutes. If the mixture dries out too much, add a little of the vegetable stock to moisten. Mash with a potato masher or pulse in a food processor to create a rough purée. Season to taste with salt and ground black pepper. Meanwhile, toss the sliced mushrooms with another 3 fl oz (85 ml) olive oil, the lemon juice, oregano and some seasoning. Grill the bread on both sides and rub with the remaining garlic clove, halved. Drizzle the bread with some more extra virgin olive oil and top with the bean purée and then the mushroom mix. Serve with a few salad leaves.

Tagliatelle with Butter and Rocket

2 handfuls of rocket leaves
(arugula or rucola)
3 spring onions, sliced
6 oz (175 g) unsalted butter
salt and ground black pepper
1 lb (450 g) fresh tagliatelle
6 basil leaves, ripped
16 black olives, stoned
freshly grated Parmesan

Tear the rocket leaves into rough pieces, removing any tough stems, then place in a large bowl with the spring onions. Melt the butter and pour over the rocket leaves. Meanwhile, in a large saucepan of boiling salted water, cook the pasta for 2-3 minutes until *al dente*. Drain the pasta and pour on to the rocket and butter. The heat of the pasta will cook and wilt the rocket leaves. Fold in the basil and black olives, season to taste and serve with a big bowl of Parmesan.

AUTUMN MENUS

THE BRITISH NURSERY	Oyster Cream Stewed Cheese
SNACKING IN THE MED	Artichoke, Aubergine and Courgette Frittata Grilled Figs with Mustard Fruits and Mascarpone
USEFUL LEFTOVERS	Chicken Noodle Soup A Weekday Scrabble
A CLASS APART	White Truffled Mash Diver Scallops with Bacon Greens
THE MUFFIN MAN	Fresh Broccoli and Pear Juice Dried Cherry Muffins
A CRAB FESTIVAL	Chilli-corn Crab Cakes Crab Fettucine
MAKING SENSE OUT OF YOUR VEGETABLES	Wild Mushroom Salad with Baby Spinach Fettucine with Tomatoes, Basil and Garlic
THE BRITISH BRUNCH	Butter-crumbed Eggs on Sorrel Devilled Lambs' Kidneys
FISH: NO BONES ATTACHED	Buckling with Apples and Horseradish Old-fashioned Fish and Corn Chowder
SKY-HIGH PICNIC	Goat's Cheese with Red Pepper and Aubergine Prawn and Sweetcorn Salad
ONE-POT DINING	Leek and Mascarpone Risotto
SIMPLY THE BEST	Pan-fried Red Mullet with Tomatoes and Herbs Mango Cream with Mango Sauce

SOCIABLE SNACKS	Vodka-soaked Cherry Tomatoes
	Mini Yorkshire Puddings with Roast Beef and
	Horseradish Cream
	My Favourite Sandwich
SOPHISTIKIDS	Spaghetti Carbonara
	Fennel, Mushroom and Parmesan Salad
BIG WITH BREAD	Big Garden Loaf
	Bruschetta with Mascarpone and Fresh Figs
POMMES OU POMMES DE TERRE?	Smoked Haddock and Potato 'Risotto'
	Panettone 'Pizza' with Fried Apples
THERE ARE TIMES WHEN ONLY JUNK WILL DO	Zapped Tomato Soup with Corn Cakes
	Driving with Your Dog
HAVING FUN WITH GARLIC	Garlic, Prune and Bacon Salad
	Garlic and Lemon Chicken with Sugar Snap Peas
ENJOYING THE MEDITERRANEAN BOUNDARIES	Aubergine with Yogurt and Tomato
	Batter-fried Mussels with Turkish Tarator Sauce
TWO OF MY FAVOURITES	Mussel and Clam Salad
	Spinach Linguine with Gorgonzola
PIZZA PROMISE	Potato, Bacon and Rosemary Pizza
	Hot Butterscotch Pecan Sauce
BREAKFAST MEETS DINNER	Spicy Mushrooms on Toast
	Lambs' Kidneys with Noodles
AUTUMN NIGHTS	Pan-fried Shrimps in a Green Curry
	Apple Calvados Risotto
A PUMPKIN FOR EATING	Pumpkin and White Bean Soup
	Pumpkin and Sausage Casserole

GROUSE ON THE CHEAP	'Quickie' Grouse
	Celeriac Bread Sauce
'R' IS FOR OYSTERS	Oyster Cocktail
	Croustade of Oysters with Melted Cheese
THE NOSH BAR	A Quickie Macaroni Cheese
	Chicory Salad with Walnuts and Croûtons
SAYING GOODBYE TO THE BARBIE	Scallops and Bacon on Sweet and Sour Cabbage
	Chargrilled Bananas with Toffee Sauce
NOT FOR THE OYSTER PURIST	Oyster Stew
	Steak Tartare with Butter-fried Oysters
MUSSELING IN ON AUTUMN	A Warm Salad of Potatoes and Wild Mushrooms
	Mussels with Cream and Basil
HEADING FOR WINTER	Woodcock in a Hurry
	Toffee Bread Pudding
IN THE MOOD FOR A QUICKIE?	Spicy Avocado Soup
	Roast Salmon with Extra Virgin Olive Oil
FOCUS ON EGGS	Egg Mayonnaise
	Scotch Woodcock with a Twist
	Shirred or Baked Eggs

THE BRITISH NURSERY

(SERVES 4)

Many of you scorn British food but, in essence, there are some wonderful foods fit for the table and for restaurants. I am managing director of an old City gem, Simpson's of Cornhill, a restaurant that serves traditional nosh; all-British, nursery food for adults. One of the savouries that outsells most is stewed cheese; another dish that can be served as a savoury or starter is oyster cream.

Oyster Cream

24 oysters, shucked
¾ pint (450 ml) double cream
1 bunch chives, snipped
1 tbsp lemon juice
pinch cayenne pepper
4 sprigs chervil

Retain the oyster liquor and strain it through a fine sieve to remove any flakes of shell. Reserve four of the oysters and push the remainder through a wire sieve, creating a smooth purée. Whip the cream until stiff, then fold in the oyster purée and the chives. Season to taste with cayenne, lemon juice and some of the reserved oyster juices. Serve cold in four ramekins, top each with an oyster and a sprig of chervil.

Stewed Cheese

12 oz (350 g) Double Gloucester cheese, grated
½ pint (300 ml) double cream
6 oz (175 g) unsalted butter
1 tsp English mustard
pinch mace
pinch cayenne pepper
2 egg yolks
4 slices toast

Bring a saucepan of water to the boil. Place a bowl over the water and add the cheese, cream and butter. Stir this mixture until the cheese melts and it is hot but not boiling. Season to taste with the mustard, mace and cayenne pepper. Fold in the egg yolks and continue stirring until the mixture begins to thicken. Do not boil. Pour over the slices of toast and grill if required.

SNACKING IN THE MED

(SERVES 4)

I know it's not good to pick, but I love going home and finding snacking food in the fridge. Foods that come to mind include Spanish tortilla, salamis, bowls of hummus and taramasalata, chilli olives, grilled vegetable salad and frittata. One of my favourite frittatas, now that excellent roast vegetables are available in jars, is one with artichokes, aubergine and courgette. This is followed by Grilled Figs with Mustard Fruits and Mascarpone.

Artichoke, Aubergine and Courgette Frittata

4 tbsp extra virgin olive oil
1 onion, finely sliced
1 tsp soft thyme leaves
2 courgettes, finely sliced
4 tbsp diced grilled aubergine, from a jar
4 tbsp diced grilled artichoke, from a jar
2 tbsp diced sun-dried tomatoes
2 tbsp ripped basil leaves
6 eggs, lightly beaten
salt and ground black pepper
3 oz (75 g) Parmesan, freshly grated

Heat half the oil in a frying pan and cook the onion and thyme over a medium flame until the onion has softened, without colouring. Add the courgette and cook for a further 5 minutes. Tip the mixture into a colander to drain and cool, then combine with the aubergine, artichoke, sun-dried tomato and basil. Add this mixture to the beaten egg and Parmesan and season with salt and ground black pepper. Pour the remaining oil in to a 12-in (30-cm) non-stick frying pan, place over a medium heat and, when the oil is hot enough to make the egg sizzle, pour in the mixture. Stir with a fork for a couple of minutes to distribute the filling evenly. Reduce the heat and cook the frittata gently until it has set, about 15 minutes. Turn the frittata on to a large plate and serve in cubes or wedges, warm or at room temperature.

Grilled Figs with Mustard Fruits and Mascarpone

8 purple figs, halved
8 tsp Mostarda di Cremona, diced
4 oz (100 g) Mascarpone cheese
6 tsp diced sun-dried cherries
4 tbsp caster sugar (optional)

The mustard fruits can be home-made or purchased in an Italian delicatessen. Place the figs cut-side up in a shallow baking dish; top each half with a little of the mustard fruits. Top the mustard fruits with a teaspoon of Mascarpone. Scatter the dish with the diced cherries and then, if desired, sprinkle with caster sugar. Place the dish under a preheated grill until the sugar melts and the Mascarpone starts to run. Serve immediately

USEFUL LEFTOVERS
(SERVES 2)

There was a time when mother used to buy a huge joint on Sundays. Not only did it have more flavour, but she also knew she had plenty left over with which to make different dishes later in the week. Dishes may have included shepherd's pie, meat loaf, mince or meat patties. A dish I enjoy is a scrabble of roast meat, cabbage and potato, preceded by something simple like Chicken Noodle Soup, another dish for the thrifty from Sunday's leftover roast chicken.

Chicken Noodle Soup

8 oz (225 g) egg noodles
salt and ground black pepper
1 tsp sesame oil
1 tbsp vegetable oil
½ tsp grated ginger
1 clove garlic, finely chopped
½ tsp diced chilli
3 spring onions, sliced
2 tbsp soy sauce
1 tsp liquid honey
1 pint (600 ml) chicken stock
6 oz (175g) cooked chicken,
shredded (optional)
1 tbsp chopped coriander leaves

Cook the noodles in boiling salted water until tender, about 4 minutes. Meanwhile, in another saucepan heat the two oils over a medium heat. Add the ginger, garlic, chilli and spring onion and cook for 3 minutes, stirring constantly. Add the soy, honey and chicken stock, bring to the boil and simmer for 3 minutes. Season to taste. When the noodles are cooked, drain and plunge into cold water to arrest cooking. Drain again and add to the soup with the cooked chicken and coriander. Reheat for 2 minutes.

A Weekday Scrabble

2 tbsp dripping or fat from the
roasting tray
1 clove garlic, finely chopped
1 onion, finely diced
½ tsp soft thyme leaves
10 oz (275 g) leftover beef, chicken,
duck or lamb, off the bone,
cubed or shredded
2 cooked potatoes, sliced
2 handfuls shredded spring greens,
cabbage or spinach
4 tbsp leftover gravy or red wine
salt and ground black pepper

Melt the dripping in a frying pan and, when hot, add the garlic, onion and thyme. Cook over a medium heat until the onion is soft and just starting to brown. Increase the heat, add the meat and potato, and cook until the potato and meat start to crisp. Add your greens and stir-fry until the leaves have wilted. Pour in the gravy or wine, increase the heat and cook until the liquid has all but evaporated. Season to taste and serve immediately.

A CLASS APART

(SERVES 4)

Generally, in life the classes don't mix. Not that there is any reason for them not to do so; they just don't. They used to say the same about food; luxury fare not mixing with peasant nosh. Times are a-changing, after all it's not long ago that native oysters could be had for nothing — now look at their status. So this menu is a mixture of the classes: to start, delicious mashed potatoes with white truffles (yes, as a starter), followed by Diver Scallops with Bacon Greens.

White Truffled Mash

1 lb (450 g) floury potatoes, peeled and
cut into ½-in (2-cm) dice
salt and ground white pepper
2 oz (50 g) unsalted butter
2 tbsp white truffle oil
2 tbsp double cream
2 oz (50 g) white truffle, cleaned

Cook the potatoes in plenty of salted water until tender. Drain and return the potatoes to the saucepan to dry out over a gentle heat. Pass the potato through a ricer or a mouli-légumes, or mash in the normal way: no lumps please. Fold in the butter, truffle oil and cream. Season to taste. Do not beat otherwise you will end up with a sticky, elastic gloop — only the 'Frogs' like their potatoes this way. Divide the potatoes into four portions. Depending on your bank balance, grate or slice the truffles over the mash in a liberal manner. A little note on white truffles: white is to truffles what cocaine is to drugs — expensive — so allow £1500 per kilo. If your budget does not stretch this far, then at the other end of the truffle scale you have cultivated summer black truffles, but it's a bit like racing at Formula 1 level with a Lada!

Diver Scallops with Bacon Greens

12 oz (350 g) greens, such as bok choy,
spring greens, Savoy cabbage
salt and ground black pepper
2 oz (50 g) unsalted butter
½ clove garlic, mashed with a little salt
8 rashers streaky bacon,
sliced into batons
1 tbsp extra virgin olive oil
12 diver scallops, cleaned

Shred the greens finely, removing any tough stems. Cook in plenty of boiling salted water until tender; drain. Meanwhile, heat half the butter in a heavy frying pan, add the garlic and bacon and cook until the bacon has released most of its fat and is half crispy. Add the shredded greens and stir-fry for 3 minutes. Season with a touch of salt and plenty of ground black pepper. Set aside to keep warm. Just before serving, heat the remaining butter and the oil in another frying pan. Add the scallops when a drop of water skims across the surface of the fats. Fry for 45 seconds each side so that the outsides are crusty and the middles are just warm. Overcooked scallops are disgusting and akin to expensive wedges of cardboard. Serve the scallops sitting proudly on top of the wilted bacon greens.

THE MUFFIN MAN

If you mention the word muffin, I think the general reaction would be 'That's the American breakfast bun'. Wrong, it was a great favourite of the Brits, delivered fresh each morning by the muffin man in Victorian and Edwardian times. Subsequently it was nicked by the Americans who managed to save muffins from obscurity. One of the most delicious is dried cherry muffin, dried cherries fast becoming trendy in the food fashion stakes. Precede your muffin with a glass of centrifugally produced broccoli and pear juice, sounds disgusting, but it isn't ...

Fresh Broccoli and Pear Juice (per person)

2 pears, no need to peel, just wash
6 oz (175 g) broccoli, leaves removed
ice cubes

Cut the pears and broccoli to fit the feed tube. Extract juice via your centrifugal juicer. Stir and pour over ice cubes. This drink is a great way of using up the broccoli stalks as they generate more juice than the florets.

Dried Cherry Muffins (makes 10)

3 oz (75 g) dried pitted cherries
¼ pint (150 ml) buttermilk
butter for greasing
5 oz (150 g) plain flour
1½ tsp baking powder
pinch salt
2 oz (50 g) unsalted butter
3 oz (75 g) caster sugar
1 egg, lightly beaten
½ tsp grated orange rind

Preheat the oven to 180°C/350°F/Gas 4 and butter ten muffin cups. Soak the cherries in the buttermilk for 30 minutes, if you have time. I know it's breaking the rules, and it's unnecessary, but it just helps to soften the cherries. In a large bowl, sift together the flour, baking powder and salt. In a separate bowl, cream together the butter and sugar until light and fluffy. Add the egg and orange rind and combine. Make a well in the centre of the dry ingredients and spoon the cherry/buttermilk mixture into it. Add the butter and mix together with your hands until just combined. Don't overwork the batter. Heap the mixture into the muffin cups, filling them two-thirds full. Bake in the oven for about 20 minutes, or until a cocktail stick inserted into the centre comes out clean. Transfer the muffins to a wire rack to cool.

A CRAB FESTIVAL

(SERVES 6)

One thing that strikes me about Americans is their ability to enjoy themselves when it comes to food. Us Brits are still a bit retentive when relaxing with a few friends. Over there, they have clam bakes, crab boils, regular barbies and simple chill-out food. Crab cakes feature, especially on the East Coast, and they make them with lots of crab, not just crab paste mixed with white fish as I've seen over here. So this menu homes in on a mini crab festival.

Chilli-corn Crab Cakes

1 lb (450 g) white crab meat, picked over
8 oz (225 g) brown crab meat
1 chilli, finely diced
1 onion, finely diced
½ red pepper, finely diced
2 sticks celery, finely diced
1 x 200-g can corn kernels
2 tsp chopped dill
½ pint (300 ml) mayonnaise
1 tsp dry mustard powder
2 eggs, lightly beaten
12 water biscuits, made into rough crumbs
salt and ground black pepper
2 oz (50 g) unsalted butter

In a large bowl, mix together the two crab meats, chilli, onion, red pepper, celery, corn and dill. In another bowl, combine the mayonnaise, mustard and eggs. Add the crab to the mayo and mix well. Fold in a third of the biscuit crumbs and season to taste. Make the mixture into six large or twelve small patties. Coat each one in the remaining biscuit crumbs. The crab cakes can be made well ahead of this point and rested in the fridge until ready to cook. Heat half the butter in a large pan over medium heat and cook the cakes for 3 minutes each side, adding more butter if necessary.

Crab Fettucine

2 tbsp extra virgin olive oil
1 shallot, finely diced
1 tsp soft thyme leaves
2 tsp anchovy essence
¼ pint (150 ml) dry white wine
¼ pint (150 ml) fish stock
1 lb (450 g) asparagus, trimmed and cut into 1-in (2.5-cm) pieces
12 oz (350 g) white crab meat
1½ lb (675 g) fresh fettucine
2 oz (50 g) unsalted butter
juice of ½ lemon
2 tbsp chopped parsley
ground black pepper

Heat the olive oil in a heavy-bottomed frying pan, add the shallots and cook gently until soft but not brown. Add the thyme, anchovy essence, wine and fish stock and bring to the boil. Cook until the liquid has reduced by half. Meanwhile, bring a large pot of salted water to the boil. Add the asparagus and cook for 6 minutes. Drain and add to the reduced shallot liquid with the crab. Cook the fettucine in the asparagus water for about 3-4 minutes, depending on its freshness. Drain and add to the crab sauce. To finish, heat the butter in a frying pan until nutty and golden, add the lemon juice and parsley and pour over the pasta. Toss to combine. Season to taste with plenty of black pepper.

MAKING SENSE OUT OF YOUR VEGETABLES

(SERVES 2)

On one of my visits to Sainsbury's I noticed a good selection of interesting mushrooms. Perfect, I thought, for a light warm salad mixed with a few baby spinach leaves which could be served with a little Greek yogurt and a few fresh herbs. Our vegetarian lunch continues with a simple pasta of late season plum tomatoes with their favourite partner, basil. Delicious! I don't know why we give vegetarians such a hard time, this menu is perfect nosh and you don't even miss the protein!

Wild Mushroom Salad with Baby Spinach

3 tbsp extra virgin olive oil
2 cloves garlic, finely chopped
1 tsp soft thyme leaves
8 oz (225 g) wild mushrooms, such as chanterelles or cèpes, cleaned carefully
1 tbsp sherry vinegar
2 tbsp chopped parsley
salt and ground black pepper
3 oz (75 g) baby spinach leaves, washed and dried

Heat the olive oil in a frying pan, add the garlic and thyme and cook over a medium heat for 2 minutes. Add the wild mushrooms (if using cèpes, slice them first), increase the heat and cook quickly for 3 minutes. Add the sherry vinegar and the chopped parsley. Season with salt and ground black pepper. Allow to cool slightly and then toss with the spinach leaves. Serve at room temperature.

Fettucine with Tomatoes, Basil and Garlic

3 spring onions, finely sliced
2 cloves garlic, finely chopped
1 oz (25 g) unsalted butter
3 tbsp finely chopped basil
½ pint (300 ml) double cream
4 plum tomatoes, peeled, seeded and diced
12 oz (350 g) fresh fettucine
salt and ground black pepper
grated Parmesan

Bring a large pan of salted water to the boil. Meanwhile, cook the onion and garlic in the butter over a medium heat. After 3 minutes add the basil and the cream. Bring to the boil and reduce by a third. Turn off the heat and add the tomatoes. Add the fettucine to the boiling water and cook until *al dente*. Drain well and toss with the sauce. Season to taste with salt and ground black pepper. Serve with grated Parmesan.

THE BRITISH BRUNCH

(SERVES 2)

I was wandering around a British Food Festival last year and realised how rarely I pay any attention to dishes with GB connections. I've now changed all that by opening The Atrium on Millbank, a restaurant serving 'Brirish' food — the best of British and Irish — but how many of you cook for Britain at home? I've come up with a couple of British brunchy dishes. To start, Butter-crumbed Eggs on Sorrel and then Devilled Lambs' Kidneys on toast, both inspired by Jane Grigson in her book English Food. Both dishes should appeal to at least three of your senses — they're easy, they're delicious and, best of all, they're cheap.

Butter-crumbed Eggs on Sorrel

6oz (175 g) sorrel, washed and
stalks removed
salt and ground black pepper
unsalted butter
4 soft-poached eggs, trimmed of
ragged edges
2 raw eggs, beaten
3oz (75 g) fresh breadcrumbs

Cook the sorrel in a covered non-reactive saucepan over a moderate heat. No water is required as the sorrel will be wet from its washing. When it starts to bubble, stir continuously until the leaves break down into an olive-coloured purée. Season to taste and then fold in 2 oz (50 g) of butter, cut into small pieces, until you have a creamy emulsion. Dip the poached eggs in the raw egg and then roll gently in the breadcrumbs. Heat some more butter in a frying pan until foaming, then slide the eggs into the pan and fry on all sides until golden. The secret is to start with very soft poached eggs, so they don't overcook during the second process. Serve the eggs on top of the sorrel purée.

Devilled Lambs' Kidneys

6 fresh lambs' kidneys, suet removed,
or chicken livers
1 onion, finely chopped
1 clove garlic, finely chopped
2 oz (50 g) unsalted butter
2 tsp Worcestershire sauce
2 tsp grain mustard
dash Tabasco sauce
4 tbsp double cream
salt and ground black pepper

Coarsely chop the kidneys or chicken livers. Pan-fry the onion and garlic in the butter until soft but not brown, then increase the heat and add the kidneys. Fry for a further 2-4 minutes depending on how rare you like kidney. Remove the kidneys and set aside. Add the Worcestershire sauce, mustard, Tabasco and cream to the pan and boil for 3 minutes. Season to taste. Return the kidneys to the sauce and warm through. Serve on hot buttered toast.

FISH: NO BONES ATTACHED

(SERVES 6)

There's a bit of Jekyll and Hyde in all of us, and I'm no exception. This menu, on the one hand, provides you with fish for health and then, just when you're feeling really good about yourself, I blow it all by lacing the dish with cholesterol-laden cream. So what would be my answer to the critics who say I'm killing my customers? 'They'll die with a smile on their faces.' No but seriously, life's too short to worry about every little food scare that hits the headlines. So my motto is 'everything in moderation'. The menu: a creamy Buckling 'Brandade' with Apples and Horseradish followed by a winter-warming Old-fashioned Fish and Corn Chowder.

Buckling with Apples and Horseradish

3 buckling, smoked mackerel,
or kippers (filleted)
4 tsp lemon juice
2 dsp creamed horseradish
1 tsp cider vinegar
6 tbsp double cream, lightly whipped
2 apples, cored and diced
3 spring onions, finely sliced
salt and ground black pepper

Carefully remove any small bones from the fish fillets. Buckling are smoked herrings, but if you can't find any, then substitute smoked mackerel or kippers. Break the fillets up by shredding the flesh with two forks. Fold the lemon juice, horseradish and vinegar into the thick cream and combine with the apples, and spring onion. Fold this mixture into the fish flakes. Season to taste, using plenty of black pepper. Serve with toast, crostini or crispbread.

Old-fashioned Fish and Corn Chowder

4 oz (100 g) salt pork or streaky bacon,
cut into small cubes
2 onions, finely chopped
1 sprig thyme
1 bay leaf
3 potatoes, peeled and diced
2 pints (1.2 litres) clam juice or
fish stock
8oz (225 g) sweetcorn kernels,
tinned or fresh
2 lb (900 g) firm white fish fillets (cod,
haddock or monkfish), cut in chunks
1 pint (600 ml) double cream
3oz (75 g) unsalted butter
salt and ground black pepper

Cook the salt pork or streaky bacon in a frying pan until it becomes crispy and golden and the fats have been released. Remove the crispy 'bits' and set aside. In the bacon fat fry the onions until soft and golden, then add the thyme, bay leaf and potatoes and mix with the onions. Add the clam juice or stock and bring to the boil. Simmer for 10 minutes, then add the corn and the fish. Cook for a further 5 minutes before adding the cream and heating through. Do not allow to reboil. Just before serving, whisk in the butter and finish with the crispy pork and seasoning. Serve with chunks of crusty bread.

SKY-HIGH PICNIC
(SERVES 2)

I'm always very disappointed when I eat airline food. It doesn't seem to matter whether it's First Class or Economy, or whether the best chef consultant has prepared the menu, food never tastes like it should. Admittedly your taste buds are affected but, even so, the decision-makers seem to have the wrong idea about customers' needs. Perhaps they try too hard, because most of us would enjoy something simple with bundles of taste. I suggest you take a picnic. To start, some goat's cheese with a red pepper and aubergine pickle, and then some jumbo prawns with sweet corn.

Goat's Cheese with Red Pepper and Aubergine

1 tbsp sesame oil
2 tbsp corn or vegetable oil
8 oz (225 g) aubergine, cut into matchsticks
2 red peppers, cut into matchsticks
4 spring onions, thinly sliced
¼ pint (150 ml) chicken stock
1 tbsp soy sauce
1 chilli, finely chopped
1 in (2.5cm) ginger, finely chopped
1 tsp liquid honey
salt and ground black pepper
2 small goat's cheeses

Heat the oils in a frying pan. Add the aubergine, peppers and spring onion and cook over a high heat for 5 minutes. Add the remaining ingredients except for the cheese and simmer for 10 minutes. Season to taste. Refrigerate until ready for departure. Serve with the soft goat's cheese and crusty bread.

Prawn and Sweetcorn Salad

1 egg yolk
4 tbsp olive oil
1 tbsp lemon juice
1 tbsp Dijon mustard
2 tbsp snipped chives
2 tbsp snipped dill
1 tbsp sliced spring onion
12 cooked jumbo prawns, peeled
6 oz (175 g) fresh or frozen sweetcorn kernels, cooked

Whisk together the egg yolk, oil, lemon juice and mustard. Add the herbs and spring onion and combine with the prawns and sweetcorn.

ONE-POT DINING

(SERVES 6–8)

When it comes to entertaining at home, Brits are not very spontaneous. Invitations go out weeks in advance, out comes the best crockery, pressed napery and the polished silver, and then 'her indoors' spends all day labouring over the stove producing exaggerated dinner party food. That is not how it should be. Chill out, get on the phone and invite a few mates around for a bowl of nosh; one-pot dining at its best. Open a few bottles of New World wine and sit around the kitchen table enjoying the total experience rather than suffering a stressful extravaganza. Try this Leek and Mascarpone Risotto with a big bowl of bitter salad leaves and some wonderful extra virgin olive oil.

Leek and Mascarpone Risotto

3½ pints (2 litres) vegetable or chicken stock
3 oz (75 g) unsalted butter
4 leeks, white part only, sliced
1 tsp soft thyme leaves
6 oz (175 g) Mascarpone cheese
2 onions, finely diced
1 lb (450 g) arborio rice
½ pint (300 ml) dry white wine
3 oz (75 g) grated Parmesan
4 tbsp chopped parsley
salt and ground black pepper

Heat the stock. In another pan, melt half the butter, add the leeks and thyme leaves, and cook over a gentle heat for approximately 8 minutes. Add the Mascarpone and continue cooking for a further 5 minutes. Meanwhile, heat the remaining butter in a large saucepan and cook the onions for 3 minutes without browning. Add the rice and stir for 1 minute, making sure the grains of rice are well coated. Add the wine and stir until completely absorbed. Begin to add the hot stock a ladle at a time, stirring frequently. Allow each stock addition to be almost completely absorbed before adding the next. After approximately 20 minutes, add the leek mixture, the Parmesan and parsley, and stir energetically to combine. Season to taste and serve immediately with a big bowl of dressed salad leaves.

SIMPLY THE BEST

(SERVES 2)

I have a rule in my restaurant kitchens concerning the use of ingredients. Prime ingredients which are expensive are not to be played with, i.e. we should keep it simple. Chefs can have their play-time with the cheaper cuts of meat or fish, which tend to require more time, more cooking skills and more imagination. Unfortunately, the 30-minute menu time restriction denies me the chance of showing you these skills. However, no worries, simplicity is fashionable; this menu gives you red mullet with tomatoes and herbs, followed by Mango Cream with Mango Sauce.

Pan-fried Red Mullet with Tomatoes and Herbs

1 tbsp black olive purée
2 x 10-oz (275-g) red mullet, filleted
3 fl oz (85 ml) extra virgin olive oil
8 oz (225 g) tomatoes,
seeded and diced
1 tsp coarsely chopped tarragon leaves
1 tbsp chervil leaves
1 tbsp chopped basil
salt and ground black pepper
juice of 1 lime

Spread the olive purée on the flesh side of the four fish fillets. Heat 1 tbsp of the oil in a frying pan and cook the fillets, skin-side down, for 3 minutes. Turn the fillets over and cook for a further 3 minutes. Remove and keep warm. Combine the tomatoes, herbs, salt and ground black pepper. Heat the remaining oil with the lime juice in the frying pan. Add the tomato mixture and warm through. Pour this dressing over the red mullet. Serve with a leaf salad.

Mango Cream with Mango Sauce

3 egg yolks
4 oz (100 g) caster sugar
2 tbsp Kirsch
juice of 1 lime
6 fl oz (175 ml) double cream
3 mangoes, peeled, stoned and puréed

Beat the egg yolks in a bowl set over hot water with 3 oz (75 g) of the sugar until thickened. Place in the refrigerator to chill. When cool add half the Kirsch and half the lime juice. Whip the cream lightly and fold into two-thirds of the mango purée. Fold this into the egg mixture. Pour into glasses or bowls. Whisk the remaining sugar, Kirsch, lime juice and mango purée together and pour over the mango cream.

SOCIABLE SNACKS

(SERVES 4)

The 'social' season is over before it's begun; as usual I didn't have the time to escape from work to enjoy these very British pursuits. Often I make up for it later in the year and have a few friends over and enjoy a bottle, or six, and watch recorded highlights. We'll need a few TV snacks to soak up the alcohol, or add to it in the case of Louisiana's answer to Bloody Mary, Vodka-soaked Cherry Tomatoes.

Vodka-soaked Cherry Tomatoes

1 punnet cherry tomatoes
¼ pint (150 ml) chilli-flavoured vodka
juice of ½ lemon
1 tbsp dry sherry
6 drops Tabasco sauce
1 tsp Worcestershire sauce
1 sprig thyme
3 basil leaves
celery salt

Prick the tomatoes all over with a cocktail stick. Soak the tomatoes in a mixture of the next seven ingredients. Chill until ready to eat. When eating, sprinkle with celery salt. The remaining liquid can be drunk as 'shots' or used as a base for an excellent Bloody Mary.

Mini Yorkshire Puddings with Roast Beef Horseradish Cream (makes 12)

2 eggs
2½ fl oz (75 ml) milk
2½ fl oz (75 ml) water
1 garlic clove, crushed with 3 anchovies
salt and ground black pepper
4 oz (100 g) plain flour, sifted
dripping or butter
thinly sliced rare roast beef
horseradish cream

Preheat the oven to 200°C/400°F/Gas 6. Beat together the first five ingredients and leave to stand for 30 minutes, then whisk in the flour. Lightly grease twelve moulds in a mini-muffin tray. Heat the tray before dividing the batter between the twelve moulds. Cook until risen and fluffy; about 15 minutes. Spread the slices of beef thinly with horseradish cream. Roll up and pop into the Yorkshire puddings. Season with black pepper.

My Favourite Sandwich

4 slices wholemeal bread
4 oz (100 g) cream cheese
4 tsp diced red onion
4 oz (100 g) smoked salmon, sliced
4 tbsp mango chutney, puréed
4 slices crispy streaky bacon
2 tsp cocktail capers
2 tsp snipped chives
ground black pepper

Spread the bread with the cream cheese, top with red onion and smoked salmon, then add a dribble of mango chutney. Top this with crispy bacon and capers. Finish with a dusting of snipped chives and ground black pepper.

SOPHISTIKIDS

(SERVES 2)

What does a chef cook for his children? I guess I generally go with the flow. The most popular request is undoubtedly Spaghetti Carbonara; traditionally one would make it with just eggs, cheese and bacon, but they like it with a little Mascarpone or cream, so it's anything for a quiet life. It's difficult to get them to eat cooked vegetables but they'll eat any amount of raw, so I knock them up a salad of fennel shavings, mushrooms and Parmesan – Sophistikids!

Spaghetti Carbonara

4 oz (100 g) pancetta or streaky bacon, in the piece
2 cloves garlic, peeled and lightly crushed
knob of butter
1 tbsp olive oil
8 oz (225 g) spaghetti
2 eggs and 1 egg yolk
2 tbsp Mascarpone cheese or double cream
1 oz (25 g) Parmesan, freshly grated
2 tbsp chopped parsley
salt and ground black pepper

Cut the bacon into small strips. Cook the garlic in butter and oil until golden brown then discard the garlic. Add the bacon to the oil mixture and pan-fry until crisp. Meanwhile, bring plenty of salted water to the boil and cook the spaghetti until tender, but with a little bite. Mix together the eggs, Mascarpone, Parmesan and parsley. Drain the spaghetti and tip into a warm serving bowl. Immediately add the egg mixture and toss rapidly. Add the contents of the bacon pan and toss again. Season to taste.

Fennel, Mushroom and Parmesan Salad

1 small head fennel, very thinly sliced
salt and ground black pepper
3 tbsp extra virgin olive oil
2oz (50 g) clean button mushrooms, finely sliced
a good squeeze of lemon
1 chunk fresh Parmesan

Scatter the fennel over two plates. Season with salt, pepper and half the olive oil. Toss the mushrooms with the remaining oil, a squeeze of lemon and more salt and pepper. Strew this mix over the fennel, and top with shavings of Parmesan cheese. To form these shavings use a potato peeler or a cheese slicer.

BIG WITH BREAD

(SERVES 4)

Once a year we're subjected to Roughage Week, more officially known as National Bread Week. Bread, like potatoes, is very good for us, we are told – but not necessarily the way I eat it: lashings of butter topped with more butter, the peanut variety. One year maybe I'll try and be healthy for the whole week, so join me in a big garden loaf followed by bruschetta of Mascarpone and fresh figs.

Big Garden Loaf

1 small aubergine, thinly sliced
extra virgin olive oil
1 flat loaf, such as ciabatta
lemon juice
1 tbsp black olive paste
1 oz (25 g) rocket, washed and dried
8 oz (225 g) buffalo Mozzarella, thinly sliced
1 small red onion, thinly sliced
2 ripe tomatoes, thinly sliced
1 yellow pepper, seeded and cut into rounds
6 radishes, thinly sliced
a few oregano or basil leaves, ripped
salt and ground black pepper

In a frying pan over a high flame, cook the aubergines in a little olive oil until golden on both sides. Slice the loaf horizontally in two and dribble the interior with a little olive oil and lemon juice. Spread the bottom half with the olive paste and top with rocket leaves, followed by the warm aubergine. Layer the remainder of the ingredients in the order listed. Between each layer dribble with a little more olive oil, lemon juice and seasoning. Cover with the top half of the loaf, press down and cut at an angle into four sandwiches

Bruschetta with Mascarpone and Fresh Figs

8 ripe fresh figs
4 tbsp Mascarpone
1 tbsp Kirsch
1 tsp finely chopped mint
4 thick slices country bread
2 tbsp liquid honey

Dice five of the figs and fold into the Mascarpone with the Kirsch and the mint; mix to combine. Grill or toast the bread and spread with a little unsalted butter if required. Divide the Mascarpone mixture between the four slices and spread. Slice the remaining figs and place on top of the Mascarpone. Dribble with honey and eat whilst the toast is still warm.

POMMES OU POMMES DE TERRE?

(SERVES 2)

Potatoes are one of my favourite vegetables. They offer hundreds of options, but very few of us think of using them to make a sauce. Here I make a dish that ends up resembling risotto, excellent brunch fare: Smoked Haddock and Potato 'Risotto' with poached egg. I follow this with toasted panettone 'pizza' topped with fried apples and clotted cream.

Smoked Haddock and Potato 'Risotto'

1 pint (600 ml) milk
1 onion, cut in 2
1 bay leaf
12 oz (350 g) unbleached smoked haddock
1 clove garlic, finely chopped
2 spring onions, finely sliced
1 sprig thyme
2 oz (50 g) unsalted butter
2 medium potatoes, peeled and cut into ¼-in (5-mm) dice
2 oz (50 g) Parmesan, freshly grated
salt and ground black pepper
4 poached eggs

Heat the milk in a saucepan with the onion and bay leaf. When simmering, add the fish and cook for 8 minutes. Remove the fish and set aside; strain the cooking liquor. Cook the garlic, spring onion and thyme in half the butter for 3 minutes, then add the potato and ¾ pint (450 ml) of the cooking liquor; cook until the potatoes are tender, about 10 minutes. Flake the smoked haddock and fold into the potato mixture. Fold in the Parmesan and remaining butter. Season to taste. Warm through the poached eggs and place two on each warm plate. Top with the smoked haddock 'risotto'.

Panettone 'Pizza' with Fried Apples

3 Cox's Orange Pippin apples, peeled
1 oz (25 g) unsalted butter
1 tbsp lemon juice
2 oz (50 g) soft brown sugar
pinch ground cinnamon
pinch powdered cloves
2 slices Panettone, cut across in a 1-in (2.5-cm) 'Pizza'
2 fl oz (50 ml) clotted cream
icing sugar

Core the apples and cut each into six wedges. Pan-fry the apple in butter and lemon juice for 5 minutes. Add the brown sugar, cinnamon and cloves; continue to cook until the apple is soft and the sugar resembles toffee. Meanwhile, toast each slice of Panettone on both sides under the grill. Top with the apples, a dollop of clotted cream and sprinkle with icing sugar.

THERE ARE TIMES WHEN ONLY JUNK WILL DO
(SERVES 4)

In Paris walking the streets supping up the atmosphere, I was suddenly grabbed by an attack of the munchies. In the distance I spied a hot dog stand. Now I know one doesn't usually go to Paris for a hot dog but there are times when only junk food will do. Although the following recipes are chef inspired, they're still a little junky.

Zapped Tomato Soup with Corn Cakes

2 oz (50 g) instant polenta
½ pint (300 ml) water
3 oz (75 g) unsalted butter
6 oz (175 g) plain flour
½ tsp baking powder
good pinch bicarbonate of soda
salt and ground black pepper
2 eggs, lightly beaten
¼ pint (150 ml) milk
3 tbsp soured cream
1 tbsp liquid honey
4 oz (100 g) corn kernels, fresh or frozen
4 spring onions, sliced
vegetable oil
2 cans Heinz tomato soup
1 tsp Tabasco sauce
2 tbsp double cream

Combine the polenta and water in a saucepan and cook, stirring constantly, until thick (about 3-5 minutes). Fold in half the butter and allow the mixture to cool for 5 minutes. In a mixing bowl, combine the flour, baking powder, bicarbonate of soda and a pinch of salt. In another bowl, stir together the eggs, milk, soured cream and honey; fold into the polenta. Mix with the dry ingredients, the corn and the spring onion. Lightly oil a non-stick frying pan and cook a tablespoon of the mixture over a medium heat. After 1 minute, when the edges are cooked and the top is beginning to bubble, turn over and cook for a further minute; repeat with the remaining mixture. Meanwhile, heat the soup and fold in the Tabasco, ½ tsp black pepper, the cream and the remaining butter. Serve with the corn cakes.

Driving with Your Dog

4 hot dogs or frankfurters
4 Kraft cheese slices
4 slices streaky bacon
4 croissants or hot dog buns
4 tbsp chilli relish

Cut lengthways three-quarters of the way through the hot dog, stuff with a cheese slice and wrap in a slice of bacon. Tightly wrap each dog in a piece of kitchen foil and place in a secure spot in the hottest part of your car engine and drive for 30 minutes or longer. When peckish, remove from engine, unwrap, and place each dog in a bun. Top with relish and eat with a contented smile.

Vodka-soaked Cherry Tomatoes

Mini Yorkshire Puddings with Roast Beef and Horseradish Cream

Pan-fried Shrimps in a Green Curry

Steak Tartare with Butter-fried Oysters

HAVING FUN WITH GARLIC

(SERVES 4)

We're doing garlic again, it's such a great product. It keeps away vampires and people you don't like and, more to the point, it has the benefit of being great for your bodily health. There's so much you can do with it — bake whole bulbs slowly in the oven and spread the resulting candied cloves on hot bread, or have this garlic menu, preferably shared with your partner and two other close friends.

Garlic, Prune and Bacon Salad

6 oz (175 g) cream cheese
2 cloves garlic, crushed with a little salt
1 bunch chives, snipped
2 tbsp chopped parsley
salt and ground black pepper
16 pitted prunes, plumped in tea
16 garlic cloves, roasted until golden
8 slices streaky bacon, cut in half
3 tbsp extra virgin olive oil
2 tsp lemon juice
4 oz (100 g) baby spinach leaves

Combine the cream cheese, garlic purée, snipped chives and chopped parsley; season to taste. Stuff this cheese mixture into the prunes in the incision created by the vacated prune stone; add a roasted peeled garlic clove to each prune. Wrap a strip of bacon around each prune and skewer with a wooden cocktail stick. Pan-fry in a little of the olive oil until the bacon is crisp, then remove the cocktail sticks and keep warm. Deglaze the prune pan with the remaining olive oil, scraping all the enjoyable grungy bits from the bottom. Add lemon juice and season. Toss the spinach leaves in this dressing until the leaves start to wilt. Serve immediately on to four warm plates, and top with the prunes.

Garlic and Lemon Chicken with Sugar Snap Peas

8 chicken thighs
4 tbsp olive oil
salt and ground black pepper
20 unpeeled garlic cloves
1lb (450 g) sugar snap peas, topped and tailed
2 oz (50 g) unsalted butter
2 cloves garlic, finely chopped
2 tbsp flaked almonds
grated rind and juice of 1 lemon

Preheat the oven to 220°C/425°F/Gas 7. Rub the chicken thighs with half the olive oil and some salt and pepper; place them on top of the 20 whole garlic cloves, skin-side down. Bake in the oven for 10 minutes, then turn over and continue for a further 10 minutes or until the skin is brown. Remove the chicken and keep warm. Press the baked garlic through a sieve and spread the purée over the chicken. Meanwhile, blanch the peas for 1 minute in boiling salted water, drain and add to the chicken pan with the butter and remaining olive oil. Fold in the chopped garlic, flaked almonds, and lemon rind. Season to taste with lemon juice, salt and plenty of ground black pepper. Return the chicken thighs to the pan and combine with the peas. Serve immediately.

ENJOYING THE MEDITERRANEAN BOUNDARIES

(SERVES 4)

Mediterranean food has been in vogue for a few years now, but fashions undoubtedly move on. Many people assume the Med to be Italy or the South of France, and tend to forget all the other wonderful cuisines that come from this area. My restaurants are developing East and South to include Lebanon, Turkey and Morocco. Here we have a couple of easy snippets to whet your appetite for future fashion.

Aubergine with Yogurt and Tomato

1lb (450 g) aubergine, peeled and cut in
2-in (5-cm) cubes
1 tbsp extra virgin olive oil
1lb (450 g) plum tomatoes, peeled,
seeded and cubed
6 fl oz (175 ml) tomato juice
2 green chillies, finely diced
juice of ½ lemon
1 tbsp chopped garlic, crushed with
1 tsp salt
4 tbsp white wine vinegar
salt and ground black pepper
6 fl oz (175 ml) thick yogurt
4 spring onions, finely sliced
2 tbsp chopped parsley

Place the aubergine in an ovenproof baking dish with the olive oil, tomatoes, tomato juice, chilli and lemon juice. Cook over a medium heat for 10 minutes. Fold in the garlic paste and the vinegar and continue to cook for a further 10 minutes. Season. Stir in the yogurt and sprinkle with the spring onion and parsley. Serve warm or at room temperature with pitta bread or as a vegetable accompaniment to grilled fish or meat.

Batter-fried Mussels with Turkish Tarator Sauce

1 oz (25 g) fresh yeast
11 fl oz (325 ml) light beer
4 oz (100 g) flour
salt
2 oz (50 g) pine nuts
4 oz (100 g) stale bread, cubed, soaked
in water and squeezed dry
2 garlic cloves, mashed with salt
2 tbsp lemon juice
2 tbsp extra virgin olive oil
salt and ground black pepper
40 large cooked mussels, shells removed
vegetable oil for deep-frying
lemon wedges

Make a batter by combining the yeast with a little beer until smooth, then adding the remaining beer and the flour little by little until the consistency of double cream is achieved. Season and allow to rest in a warm place for about 20 minutes. Meanwhile, place the pine nuts in a food processor and blitz until finely ground. Add the bread and garlic; pulse a few times to make a paste. With the machine running, add the lemon juice and olive oil. Season to taste and set aside. Dust the mussels with extra plain flour and dip them in the batter; deep-fry a few at a time in hot vegetable oil until golden, 1-2 minutes. Garnish with lemon wedges and serve with the Tarator Sauce.

TWO OF MY FAVOURITES

(SERVES 4)

Mussels and Gorgonzola are two of my favourite ingredients, although not together; but in a menu they create an exciting experience. We start with a Mussel and Clam Salad. If clams are unavailable, don't make any other substitutes, as mussels on their own are great. To follow, one of the quickest pasta dishes I know, Spinach Linguine with Gorgonzola.

Mussel and Clam Salad

¼ pint (150 ml) dry white wine
1 clove garlic, finely chopped
2 shallots, finely chopped
1 sprig thyme
2¼ lb (1 kg) small clams, washed
2¼ lb (1 kg) mussels, washed
4 tbsp olive oil
1 tbsp lemon juice
salt and ground black pepper
1 red onion, finely diced
2 tomatoes, seeded and diced
⅓ cucumber, peeled and diced
2 tbsp chopped parsley
2 tbsp chopped coriander
salad leaves

In a large saucepan bring the wine, garlic, shallots and thyme to the boil. Add the clams, cover and cook for 3 minutes. Add the mussels and cook for a further 3 minutes. Remove the clams and mussels from the pan and allow to cool. Discard any that have not opened. Boil the remaining liquid until about 4 tbsp remain. Strain the liquid into a bowl, add the olive oil and lemon juice; season to taste. Remove the mussels and clams from their shells and combine with the vegetables and herbs. Toss with the dressing. Serve on a bed of salad leaves.

Spinach Linguine With Gorgonzola

1 pint (600 ml) double cream
8 oz (225 g) Gorgonzola cheese, cut into cubes
3 tbsp grated Parmesan
1 tsp ground black pepper
1 lb (450 g) fresh linguine
4 oz (100 g) unsalted butter
4 oz (100 g) baby spinach, washed
1 tsp soft thyme leaves

In a saucepan, reduce the cream over a high heat until just over half of it remains. Fold in the Gorgonzola and stir until completely melted. Add the Parmesan and pepper and stir. Check seasoning, but the sauce should not need salt. In abundant salted boiling water, cook the pasta until tender but still with a little bite. While the pasta is cooking, heat the butter in another saucepan, add the spinach and thyme, and stir until the spinach has wilted. Add the spinach and butter to the sauce. Drain the pasta and add to the sauce. Mix well to combine, then serve.

PIZZA PROMISE

(SERVES 4)

We all love a pizza, it's the perfect munching food for an evening in; log fire, good movie, what more can you ask for? Delivered pizzas are often disappointing, and the varieties available from the supermarket are, although improving, pretty grim. You don't want to be making pizza dough, so here's a compromise: buy a pizza base, roll it a little thinner and put on your own topping. Follow this with a tub of your favourite ice cream with hot butterscotch pecan sauce.

Potato, Bacon and Rosemary Pizza

6 oz (175 g) thick smoked streaky bacon rashers
4 x 7-in (18-cm) pizza bases
3 tbsp extra virgin olive oil
Maldon sea salt and ground black pepper
6 oz (175 g) buffalo Mozzarella, diced
12 oz (350 g) potatoes, washed and thinly sliced
1 tbsp chopped rosemary leaves
3 oz (75 g) Parmesan, freshly grated

Preheat the oven to its hottest setting. Slice the bacon into ¼-in (5-mm) strips, then cook them over a moderate heat in a frying pan until some of the fat has been released but the bacon is not crisp. Brush the pizza bases with olive oil and scatter with a little Maldon sea salt and ground black pepper. Divide the Mozzarella evenly over the four bases and arrange the potato slices, slightly overlapping, on top. Spread the bacon pieces and their reduced fat over the potato and finish off with the rosemary and Parmesan. Drizzle with the remaining olive oil and bake in the oven for 12-15 minutes or until the potatoes are cooked and the bases golden.

Hot Butterscotch Pecan Sauce

8 oz (225 g) soft brown sugar
4 tbsp golden syrup
2 oz (50 g) unsalted butter
salt
¼ pint (150 ml) double cream
1 tsp vanilla essence
dash lemon juice
3 tbsp dark rum
4 oz (100 g) toasted pecans, chopped

In a small heavy saucepan, mix together the brown sugar, syrup, butter and a pinch of salt. Over a medium heat, cook this mixture until the sugar has dissolved, then boil it without stirring for 14 minutes. From time to time wash down any sugar crystals that cling to the side of the saucepan with a pastry brush dipped in cold water. Remove the pan from the heat, cover your hands with a tea-towel and fold in the cream, vanilla, lemon juice, rum and pecans. Beware, as the sauce will react angrily and give you a good splattering. Serve hot, but not boiling.

BREAKFAST MEETS DINNER

(SERVES 2)

There are times when adults go through a period of needing some reminder of simpler times. These needs are sentiments of comfort, and things on toast come to mind: it could be baked beans, scrambled eggs, tomatoes and bacon or these spicy mushrooms that satisfy. Follow this with another comfort dish, and a cheap one at that, lambs' kidneys with buttery noodles.

Spicy Mushrooms on Toast

1 onion, finely diced
1 tsp grated ginger
1 clove garlic, finely diced
1 chilli, finely diced
1 tbsp sesame oil
2 tbsp vegetable oil
10 oz (275 g) button mushrooms, quartered
¼ pint (150 ml) dry white wine
1 tbsp liquid honey
1 tbsp Katchup Manis
(Indonesian sweet soy sauce)
salt and ground black pepper
2 slices granary bread
2 spring onions, sliced
1 tbsp chopped coriander
1 tbsp chopped mint
2 tbsp Greek yogurt

Over a moderate heat, cook the onion, ginger, garlic and chilli in the two oils until the onion is soft. Increase the temperature, add the mushrooms and cook for 5 minutes. Add the wine, honey and Katchup Manis and cook for a further 5 minutes. Season to taste. Toast the bread. With a slotted spoon, lift the mushrooms and place them on the toast. Boil the juices remaining in the pan until no more than 4 tbsp remain. Pour these juices over the mushrooms, scatter with spring onions, coriander and mint, and top with a good dollop of yogurt.

Lambs' Kidneys with Noodles

4 lambs' kidneys, sliced in 2
¼ pint (150 ml) chicken stock
4 oz (100 g) unsalted butter, cut in cubes
12 oz (350 g) fresh fettucine
salt and ground black pepper
1 tbsp olive oil
1 clove garlic, finely diced
3 oz (75 g) spinach leaves, washed
3 tbsp mixed soft herbs, such as
tarragon, chives, parsley

Remove all the fat and membrane from the centre of each kidney and cut each half into three. Heat the stock and whisk in the butter pieces, creating a smooth emulsion. Keep warm. In a pan of boiling salted water cook the pasta until ready; drain well. Meanwhile, pan-fry the kidneys in hot oil with the garlic for about 4 minutes; the kidneys should be rosy in the centre. To the kidneys add the spinach and herbs and cook until wilted. Season to taste. Toss the pasta in the buttery stock emulsion, then fold in the kidney mixture. Serve immediately.

AUTUMN NIGHTS

(SERVES 4)

I think we can safely say that summer is definitely over; some autumn nights could freeze the nuts off a brass monkey! The time has come for big bowls of warming foods. I start with some grilled shrimps in a Thai-inspired curry sauce and follow it with a sacrilegious version of an Italian risotto.

Pan-fried Shrimps in a Green Curry

½ pint (300 ml) coconut cream
3 tbsp vegetable oil
24 uncooked jumbo shrimps, shelled
2 cloves garlic, finely chopped
1 chilli, finely chopped
1 tbsp grated ginger
2 tbsp green Thai curry paste
¼ pint (150 ml) vegetable stock
2tbsp nam pla (Thai fish sauce)
2 tsp caster sugar
20 basil leaves, ripped
3 oz (75 g) baby spinach leaves

In a small saucepan heat the coconut cream, but do not let it boil. In another pan, heat the vegetable oil and fry the shrimps for 1 minute each side; remove and keep warm. Add the garlic, chilli and ginger to the pan and fry until golden. Add the curry paste and cook for a few more seconds, then pour in the coconut cream and stir until the sauce separates and thickens. Add the stock, fish sauce and sugar and bring to the boil. Cook for a further 2 minutes, then fold in the shrimps, basil leaves and spinach. Serve with buttered noodles.

Apple Calvados Risotto

3oz (75 g) unsalted butter
4 small Granny Smith apples, peeled, cored and cut into ½-in (1-cm) dice
4 tbsp sugar
4 tbsp Calvados
12 oz (350 g) arborio rice
1 sprig thyme
1tsp vanilla extract
2½ pints (1.4 litres) unsweetened apple juice, hot
10 oz (275 g) Mascarpone cheese
scant 2 oz (50 g) almonds or walnuts, toasted and coarsely chopped

Heat half the butter until frothing in a small frying pan, add the apples and sugar and cook fast until the apples are tender and caramelised, about 10 minutes. Add half the Calvados, stir to combine, and keep warm. Meanwhile, melt the remaining butter in a large saucepan, add the rice and thyme, and cook for about 2 minutes until the rice is translucent. Add the vanilla extract, then the hot apple juice ladle by ladle; allow the liquid to be absorbed before each new addition. Cook until the rice is tender, about 20 minutes. Stir in half the apple mixture and the Mascarpone. Serve in a large bowl and top with the remaining apple and a scattering of nuts. Heat the remaining Calvados, ignite, and pour over the risotto. Serve with extra Mascarpone or clotted cream.

A PUMPKIN FOR EATING
(SERVES 4)

It's Halloween and in sunny Britain we don't celebrate it as wildly as they do in America. We Brits tend to associate this occasion with carved candle-lit pumpkins – a pity as this vegetable has great culinary possibilities. Unfortunately most recipes tend to take longer than our allotted 30 minutes, but I've dug up a couple which can be done in the time: a Pumpkin and White Bean Soup and Pumpkin and Sausage Casserole.

Pumpkin and White Bean Soup

1 small pumpkin, peeled, seeded and diced
2 leeks, white part only, finely sliced
1 carrot, finely diced
2 sticks celery, finely diced
2 cloves garlic, finely diced
4 sage leaves, shredded
2 tbsp good olive oil
2 pints (1.2 litres) chicken or vegetable stock
1 x 420-g can cannelini beans, drained
2 tbsp grated Parmesan
2 tbsp chopped parsley
salt and ground black pepper

Pan-fry the vegetables, garlic and sage in the olive oil for approximately 7 minutes. Pour in the stock and bring to the boil, lower heat and simmer for 15 minutes. Add the beans, heat through, then fold in the Parmesan and parsley. Season to taste. If you don't like a chunky soup this can be liquidised and thinned down with a little stock or cream.

Pumpkin and Sausage Casserole

1 onion, roughly chopped
2 cloves garlic, roughly chopped
1 red pepper, roughly chopped
1 chilli, finely diced
1 tsp thyme leaves
2 tbsp olive oil
12 oz (350 g) chorizo sausage, cut into ⅛-in (3-mm) rounds
1 small pumpkin, peeled, seeded and cut into ½-in (1-cm) cubes
2 tbsp balsamic vinegar
salt and ground black pepper
Greek yogurt

Pan fry the onion, garlic, red pepper, chilli and thyme in the olive oil until the onion has started to soften. Add the sausage and pumpkin and cook, stirring frequently, until the pumpkin is tender, about 10 minutes. Add the vinegar and stir to combine. Season with salt and ground black pepper. Serve each portion topped with a dollop of Greek yogurt.

GROUSE ON THE CHEAP

(SERVES 2)

Grouse is fairly abundant now and the prices associated with the Glorious Twelfth have dropped considerably. Prices take time to reach sensible proportions. Imagine, on the opening day of the season I needed a pair of grouse to cook on the Richard Littlejohn Show, and I was quoted over a £100 a brace by some dealers. Expect to pay between £5 and £6 a bird.

'Quickie' Grouse

2 spatchcocked grouse
salt and ground black pepper
2 oz (50 g) unsalted butter
4 slices streaky bacon
2 slices white bread
1 shallot, finely chopped
1 tsp soft thyme leaves
4 oz (100 g) chicken livers, finely chopped
3 fl oz (85 ml) Calvados
1 tbsp redcurrant jelly

Spatchcock means asking your game dealer to split the birds down the backbone and flatten them out; presumably they are supposed to resemble a spatchcock (whatever that may be), but to me they look more like a rather plump butterfly. Preheat the oven to 200°C/400°F/Gas 6. Fry the seasoned birds skin-side down in half the butter until brown, flip over and pop into the oven, for 8 minutes. Meanwhile, fry the bacon until crispy, remove and keep warm. In the same pan, fry the bread on both sides in the bacon fat until golden, then remove and keep warm. In another pan, cook the shallot and thyme in the remaining butter over a medium heat until soft but not brown. Increase the heat and add the chicken livers (if you wish you can use the grouse liver as well) and cook for a further 2 minutes. Season to taste. Remove and place on top of the fried bread. Add the Calvados and redcurrant jelly to the chicken liver pan and stir until melted. Place the grouse on top of the chicken liver and pour over the sauce. Serve with crispy bacon, celeriac bread sauce (see below), a watercress salad and a few warm crisps.

Celeriac Bread Sauce

½ celeriac, peeled and cut into 1-in (2.5-cm) cubes
2 shallots, roughly chopped
½ pint (300 ml) milk
2 cloves
1 bay leaf
pinch grated nutmeg
2 oz (50 g) fresh white breadcrumbs
2 oz (50 g) unsalted butter
4 tbsp double cream
salt and ground black pepper

Boil the celeriac and shallot in the milk with the herbs and spices for 10 minutes. Add the breadcrumbs and cook until the celeriac is tender. Pass this mixture through a food mill or blend in a food processor (remove cloves and bay leaf before blending). Fold in the butter and double cream and season to taste. If the mixture is too thin, return to the heat and cook until the right consistency is obtained.

'R' IS FOR OYSTERS

(SERVES 2)

The 'R' in the month means our exciting shellfish season is with us again. While helping with the judging for the Tabasco Oyster Opening Championship recently, it struck me how lucky we are to have so many indigenous products available from our shores. It certainly makes a big change from a recent holiday in central Italy where the only shellfish available seems to be frozen. How about kicking the season off with a knockout Oyster Cocktail (yes, you drink it), followed by a Croustade of Oysters with Melted Cheese.

Oyster Cocktail (per person)

½ dozen small oysters, shucked
1 dash lemon juice
1 tsp tomato sauce
2 dashes Worcestershire sauce
2 dashes Champagne vinegar
2 dashes Tabasco sauce
salt and ground black pepper

Combine the first six ingredients and season with a little salt and pepper. Stir gently with a spoon and serve in a Champagne glass. If you're brave, knock it back in one hit ... a great way to cure a hangover!

Croustade of Oysters with Melted Cheese

12 slices bread, crusts removed
4 oz (100 g) unsalted butter, melted
4 slices streaky bacon, roughly chopped
4 spring onions, finely sliced
3 fl oz (85 ml) dry white wine
3oz (75 g) grated Emmenthal cheese
pinch nutmeg
2 tbsp snipped chives
2 tbsp chopped parsley
1 tsp soft thyme leaves
12 oysters, shucked
paprika

Preheat the oven to 180°C/350°F/Gas 4. Flatten the bread slices with a rolling pin, cut into 3-in (7.5-cm) circles and brush one side with half the melted butter. Press the buttered side down into mini-muffin or Yorkshire pudding moulds and bake in the oven for 8 minutes. Meanwhile, fry the bacon until crisp, remove and keep warm. In the same pan, fry the spring onions until wilted, add the wine and bring to the boil, then remove from the heat and fold in the cheese and nutmeg, stirring until melted. Add the chives, parsley, thyme and crispy bacon and stir to combine. Heat the remaining butter in a frying pan and cook the oysters for 30 seconds each side. Place one oyster in each croûstade and top with the cheese mixture. Bake in the oven for about 5 minutes, until golden and bubbling. Dust with paprika and serve immediately with a green salad.

THE NOSH BAR

(SERVES 2)

Perfect Sunday night nosh: with the autumn weather which can be severe, it's time for supper in front of a big log fire, a good bottle of red wine, and macaroni cheese served with a light salad. This macaroni quickie stems from a dish cooked by the French. I serve it with a chicory salad (any other leaves could be substituted). The dressing is made with walnut oil, a survivor amongst the trendy oils so popular in nouvelle cuisine days.

A Quickie Macaroni Cheese

6 oz (175 g) macaroni
1½ pints (900 ml) chicken stock or
salted water
½ onion, finely diced
1 tsp soft thyme leaves
1 oz (25 g) unsalted butter
4 oz (100 g) country ham, diced
½ tbsp tomato purée
6 oz Gruyère or Cantal cheese, grated
2 egg yolks
salt and ground black pepper

Cook the macaroni to *al dente* in boiling seasoned stock or water. Meanwhile, sweat the onion and thyme in the butter until soft but not brown. Add the ham and tomato purée. Allow to cool slightly. Drain the macaroni and mix with three-quarters of the cheese. Beat the egg yolks and stir into the macaroni. Finally fold in the ham mixture. Check the seasoning and then top with the remainder of the cheese. Brown under the hot grill until golden.

Chicory Salad with Walnuts and Croûtons

2 heads chicory
2 tbsp vegetable oil
1 clove garlic, diced
1 slice country bread, cut into croûtons
2 tbsp walnut oil
8 walnuts, whole
1 tbsp aged sherry vinegar
salt and ground black pepper
2 tbsp snipped chives

Separate the leaves from the chicory and only wash if necessary. Retaining a dozen whole leaves, shred the remainder, then set aside. In a frying pan, heat the vegetable oil, add the garlic and the croûtons and fry until golden. Remove the croûtons from the oil and add the shredded chicory, along with the walnut oil and walnuts. Cook for 1 minute and then add the sherry vinegar. Season to taste. Toss the chicory in this warm dressing with the chives. Serve immediately, garnishing with the whole chicory leaves.

SAYING GOODBYE TO THE BARBIE

(SERVES 4)

Say goodbye to the sun in style, it's that time again when the barbie gets an autumn clean and prepares itself for winter hibernation. For those last rays of sunshine, there's a treat in store … some chunky scallops fresh from the shell, served with crispy bacon and sweet and sour cabbage. Order 'real' scallops from your fishmonger, not frozen or prepared, as these tend to be pumped up with water which hinders the chargrilling, giving a boiled result instead of a crusty, golden exterior. To follow, a deliciously simple pud of chargrilled bananas served with a gungy moreish sauce, a dish inspired by Michael Coaker, Executive Chef at the Mayfair Hotel.

Scallops and Bacon on Sweet and Sour Cabbage

1 Savoy cabbage, trimmed and shredded
1 egg yolk
½ onion, finely diced
2 oz (50 g) caster sugar
3 fl oz (85 ml) cider vinegar
2 oz (50 g) unsalted butter, cut in small cubes
¼ pint (150 ml) double cream
1 tsp Dijon mustard
1 bunch dill, finely chopped
salt and ground black pepper
12 large scallops, shucked
8 rashers streaky bacon

Preheat the barbie. Cook the cabbage in boiling salted water for about 8 minutes. At the same time, whisk together the egg yolk, onion, sugar and vinegar over a low heat until it begins to thicken. Fold in the butter, then the cream, mustard and dill. Do not allow the sauce to boil. Drain the cabbage and fold into the sauce. Season to taste. Place the scallops and the bacon on to the grill and cook both for 2 minutes on each side, less if you prefer your scallops a little underdone in the centre. Serve the scallops and bacon on top of the cabbage.

Chargrilled Bananas with Toffee Sauce

4 oz (100 g) unsalted butter
4 oz (100 g) soft brown sugar
1 tsp ground cinnamon
4 fl oz (100 ml) dark rum
¼ pint (150 ml) double cream
8 bananas in their skins

Heat the butter with the sugar, cinnamon and rum; simmer until the sauce begins to thicken, stirring from time to time. Add the cream and whisk until the sauce emulsifies. Do not boil. Place the bananas, unpeeled, on the barbie and cook until the skins have blackened all over and are just beginning to split. Allow your guests to peel the bananas, serve the sauce separately, and watch for the orgasmic reactions.

NOT FOR THE OYSTER PURIST

(SERVES 2)

Here we go again, it's oyster time again. Oyster purists who wouldn't dream of eating their mollusc any other way than slip-slidingly raw should turn the page now, because my recipes in this menu require an element of cookery skills; sacrilege I know, but delicious all the same. To start with, a quickie stew and then, to follow, a reverse application of the popular Bordeaux dish of hot sausages with cold oysters: mine is raw steak, as in tartare, with butter-fried oysters.

Oyster Stew

2 oz (50 g) unsalted butter
1 tsp anchovy essence
2 tsp English mustard
2 tbsp each chopped onion and celery
1 pint (600 ml) double cream
12 rock oysters with their liquor, shucked
large splash dry sherry
salt, ground black pepper and paprika

Melt the butter in a small saucepan and add the anchovy essence, mustard, onion and celery. Cook until soft. Add the cream and bring to the boil. Add the oyster liquor, the sherry and the oysters; heat until the edges of the oysters start to curl. Season to taste and dust with paprika.

Steak Tartare with Butter-fried Oysters

10 oz (275 g) beef sirloin, trimmed of fat and finely ground
1 tbsp finely chopped spring onion
1 tbsp finely chopped flat parsley
2 tsp Dijon mustard
2 tsp chopped gherkin
1 tsp chopped capers
2 chopped anchovies
1 tsp finely diced chilli or Tabasco sauce
1 tsp Worcestershire sauce
1 raw egg yolk
½ tsp salt
1 tsp ground black pepper
2 oz (50 g) unsalted butter
12 oysters, shucked (keep the shells)

Combine the first twelve ingredients in a mixing bowl and blend with a fork until just mixed. Form into two burgers and refrigerate until ready to eat. Heat some of the butter in a frying pan until foaming, dry the oysters and add them six at a time. Cook over a fierce heat, until the edges curl, turning once. Remove, then repeat with the second six, adding extra butter as necessary. Season to taste. Place the oysters in their own shells warmed and circle them around the tartare. Serve with hot buttered toast.

MUSSELING IN ON AUTUMN

(SERVES 2)

This is the time of year when there are so many excellent products in the shops. The summery bits are out, but there's fantastic shellfish, game and wild mushrooms. Mussels are wonderfully full and fat after their summer holidays, so your main course is a variation on the theme of moules marinières. To start, a warm salad of my favourite mushrooms, cèpes – really gutsy, meaty little numbers available free if you're prepared to search the forests around our country. But beware! Make sure you know what you're picking. I'd hate you to eat some of the magic variety. Field mushrooms can be substituted if you aren't the energetic type, or you can go to Harrods or Antonio Carluccio's shop in Neal Street, Covent Garden.

A Warm Salad of Potatoes and Wild Mushrooms

4 tbsp virgin olive oil
2 shallots, finely chopped
3 cloves garlic, finely chopped
6 oz (175 g) cooked new potatoes, sliced
6 oz (175 g) cèpes or field mushrooms, wiped and sliced
3 tbsp chopped parsley
salt and ground black pepper

Heat the oil in a frying pan, add the shallots and garlic and cook until soft but not brown. Increase the heat and add the potatoes. Cook for a further 5 minutes, turning from time to time. Add the cèpes and parsley and cook until the potatoes and cèpes are golden. Season with salt and ground black pepper

Mussels with Cream and Basil

¼ pint (150 ml) dry Martini
¼ pint (150 ml) water
2 shallots, finely chopped
1 sprig of thyme
1 bay leaf
3 lb (1.4 kg) clean small mussels
¼ pint (150 ml) double cream
2 tsp pesto
salt and ground black pepper

Put the dry Martini, water, shallots, thyme and bay leaf in a large pan and bring to the boil. Cover and simmer for 10 minutes. Add the mussels, cover tightly and boil for 3-5 minutes, shaking vigorously from time to time. When the mussels open, remove and keep them warm. Discard any mussels that haven't opened. Strain the juices through a fine sieve into another saucepan, and boil furiously until the liquid has reduced by half. Pour in the cream and boil for a further 5 minutes. Finally, fold in the pesto, stir to combine and season to taste. Pour over the mussels and serve immediately with some crusty bread.

HEADING FOR WINTER

(SERVES 4)

Have you ever tried woodcock? No? Well you should, it has to be the best game bird going. It has lots of flavour without having to be subjected to the degrading practice of hanging until it goes green. And another gem of information, this is one of only two birds (the other being snipe) where you can eat its entire innards. Interested to learn more? Apparently woodcock go to the loo every time they take off, hence the clean insides. Fascinating. Plain roast, just a croûton spread with foie gras, a green vegetable and some game crisps – delicious. To follow, a quick, grungy, Toffee Bread Pudding.

Woodcock in a Hurry

4 woodcock, uncleaned, heads removed
4 slices streaky bacon
6 juniper berries
1 sprig thyme
1 onion, cut in quarters
4 cloves garlic
2 bay leaves
1 carrot, sliced
¼ pint (150 ml) red wine
2 tbsp redcurrant jelly
½ pint (300 ml) beef stock
2 oz (50 g) unsalted butter
4 slices white country bread, toasted
4 slices pâté de foie gras

Preheat the oven to 220°C/425°F/Gas 7. Cover the woodcock with streaky bacon. Place the birds in a roasting tray with the juniper, thyme, onion, garlic, bay and carrot. Roast in the oven for 15 minutes. Remove the breasts and legs and keep them warm. Chop up the carcasses (wear an apron as this can be quite messy). Deglaze the roasting tray with the red wine and pour the contents into a saucepan with the carcasses. Add the redcurrant jelly and the stock and simmer for 10 minutes. Strain and return the juices to a saucepan. Boil vigorously and add the butter in small pieces. Warm the meat in this sauce and serve it on the toasted croûtons spread with foie gras. For those with a strong constitution, the foie gras can be replaced with mashed woodcock guts – an acquired taste.

Toffee Bread Pudding

6 oz (175 g) unsalted butter
4 tbsp golden syrup
5 oz (150 g) soft brown sugar
¾ pint (450 ml) double cream
12 slices thick cut bread, crusts removed

Preheat the oven to 180°C/350°F/Gas 4. Heat the butter, syrup and brown sugar in a saucepan, stirring until the sugar has melted. Boil for 5 minutes. Warm the cream in a separate pan. Cut the bread into soldiers. Dip each one into the warm cream. Make a layer in the bottom of a small baking dish. Pour some toffee over the bread and continue this layering until all the bread has been used up. Finish with the toffee and any remaining cream. Serve immediately or bake in the oven for 20 minutes. This pud is also excellent served cold for breakfast with sliced banana.

IN THE MOOD FOR A QUICKIE?

(SERVES 4)

What's one of the quickest soups you can knock up when someone turns up unexpectedly. The answer must be cold avocado soup, given that you've got the ingredients. Well, most people have an avocado hanging around, don't they? Another quickie, and dead cheap nowadays, is salmon fillets with a simple olive oil and tomato dressing. I like to eat the crispy skin, but this can be removed if it's objectionable.

Spicy Avocado Soup

1 can Campbell's consommé
2 ripe avocados, peeled, stoned and diced
1 chilli, finely diced
juice of 1 lime
½ tsp ground coriander
½ tsp ground cumin
8 fl oz (250 ml) double cream
salt and ground black pepper
2 tomatoes, seeded and diced
3 spring onions, sliced
1 tbsp chopped coriander leaves

In a food processor or liquidiser, blend the consommé, avocado, chilli, lime juice, coriander and cumin until smooth. Fold in the cream, stir to combine and season to taste. Add the tomato, spring onions and coriander leaves. Chill.

Roast Salmon with Extra Virgin Olive Oil

4 x 6-oz (175-g) salmon fillets
salt and ground black pepper
6 fl oz (175 ml) extra virgin olive oil
4 tomatoes, seeded and diced
3 tbsp ripped basil leaves
1 tsp balsamic vinegar
12 black olives, stoned and halved

Preheat the oven to 180°C/350°F/Gas 4. Season the salmon with salt and black pepper. Place a cast-iron skillet over a medium heat and add a little olive oil. When the oil is hot, place the salmon fillets skin-side down into the pan and cook for 3 minutes or until the skin is crisp and golden. Turn the salmon over and pop into the oven to cook for a further 8 minutes. Meanwhile, in a small saucepan, heat the remaining olive oil, then add the tomatoes and heat through. Add the basil, balsamic vinegar and seasoning. When the salmon is cooked, place the fillets in a dish and pour the tomato and olive oil mix over the steaks, garnish with the black olives. Serve with a leaf salad and some buttered new potatoes.

FOCUS ON EGGS

(SERVES 2)

Gone are the days when we emerge from the bedroom, descend the stairs to the breakfast room, and find a magnificent buffet laid out on a mahogany sideboard. But 'eggs is eggs' as they say, so here's a smattering of egg dishes, not really a menu, more a focus on eggs. Don't eat them all at once, or egg-bound you will be. The selection includes an old English favourite soon to make a come-back on restaurant menus, Egg Mayonnaise followed by Scotch Woodcock with a Twist.

Egg Mayonnaise

1 heart Little Gem lettuce
3 hard-boiled eggs, shelled
3 tbsp good mayonnaise
4 canned anchovies, drained
2 tsp salted capers, rinsed
pinch paprika
pinch cayenne pepper
1 tsp snipped chives

Arrange a bed of lettuce leaves on the bottom of two cold plates. Place three halves of egg, cut-side down on the lettuce leaves and top each with the mayonnaise. Cut the anchovies in half lengthways and lay on top of the eggs. Scatter with capers and dust with paprika, cayenne and chives.

Scotch Woodcock with a Twist

5 eggs
salt and ground black pepper
4 oz (100 g) unsalted butter
2 thick slices country bread
2 thin slices Gentlemen's Relish
(Patum Peperium)

Break the eggs into a bowl, season and beat gently with a fork (don't overbeat as scrambled eggs need to have some viscosity). In a non-stick saucepan or frying pan, melt 1½ oz (40 g) of the butter over a medium heat. When the butter is foaming, add the eggs. Stir from time to time. The French whisk their scrambled eggs constantly but I prefer a rougher texture. Add another 1½ oz (40 g) butter half-way through the cooking process. I like my eggs soft, but stop cooking them whenever suits your fancy, remembering that the eggs will continue to cook for some time after you remove them from the heat. Meanwhile, toast or grill the bread on both sides until golden, then butter each slice and top with the Gentlemen's Relish. Pour over the scrambled eggs and serve immediately. (Gentlemen's Relish is a traditional anchovy paste which in the old days formed part of the gentry's staple diet.)

Shirred or Baked Eggs

2 oz (50 g) unsalted butter
4 drops Tabasco sauce
2 tsp anchovy essence
4 tbsp double cream
ground black pepper
4 large eggs

Preheat the oven to 190°C/375°F/Gas 5. Liberally butter four ramekins. In the bottom of each put a drop of Tabasco, ½ tsp anchovy essence and 1 tbsp double cream. Season with ground black pepper; no salt is necessary as the anchovy essence should compensate. Break an egg into each ramekin and place in the oven for 10-15 minutes, depending on how hard you like your eggs.

WINTER MENUS

CAULIFLOWER: A CABBAGE WITH A COLLEGE EDUCATION	Westminster Cauli Pasta Baked Amaretti Peaches
HEALTH, COMFORT AND CRUDITÉS	Crudités with Tapénade Cheesy Potatoes with Charcuterie
SAVOURIES REVISITED	Cod's Roe Savoury Scrambled Crab Hot Cheese Pudding
FANCY A FRY-UP?	Prawn Cutlets Apple Fritters
SUBTLE IMPERSONATIONS	Pissaladière Toast A Sort of Stroganoff
SOURCING THE SAUCE	Sweet and Sour Dipping Sauce Coriander-mint Chutney Oriental Mustard Sauce
MOUNTAIN MAGIC	Hot Spiced Wine Cheese Fondue
GARLIC MISCHIEF	A Warming Garlic Soup A Bowl of Steaming Mussels
CHRISTMAS EVE COMFORT	Scallops with Hot Potato Salad Savoury Cheese Sausages
CHRISTMAS CHEER	Christmas Spirit Bacon Croissant Buttie
CHILLING ON BOXING DAY	Simple Caesar Salad Christmas Lunch Club Sandwich

CALORIE COUNTDOWN TO CHRISTMAS	Mushroom Caviar
	Spicy Shrimp and Cucumber
TIME TO BE INDULGENT	Buckwheat Blinis
	Caviar Dip
	Baked New Potatoes with Caviar
TALKING SOUFFLÉ SENSE	Creamy Sardines on Toast
	Cheese and Bacon Soufflé
SAFE FROM THE SALES	Mozzarella Skewers with Black Olive Paste
	Black Olive Paste
	A Cup of Something Hot
THINKING SLIM	Asparagus with Red Pepper Sauce
	Baked Cod with Olives and Spring Onions
RAIDING THE PANTRY	Tomato and Flageolet Bean Soup
	Macaroni with Garlic, Eggs and Bacon
TAKING CHEESE TO HEART	Cheese Soup
	Saltimbocca
NOT COMING HOME TO REALITY	Stamp and Go
	Blaff
SIMPLE LUXURIES	Eggcetera
	Wild Mushroom Sandwich
CHRISTMAS IS BUT A MEMORY	Marinated Tofu, Onion, Mushroom and Bok Choy
	Spaghetti with Herby Green Sauce
SIMPLY VALENTINE	New Potatoes with Soured Cream and Caviar
	Rock and Native Oysters
	Boiled Lobster with Asparagus
	Haagen-Dazs Ice Cream

THE MALE VALENTINE Lobster Hearts with Coriander Oil
Sexy Toffee Pudding

A NEW START TO MORNING MUNCHING Muesli with Bananas and Coconut
Crispy Bacon Hash

CAULIFLOWER: A CABBAGE WITH A COLLEGE EDUCATION
(SERVES 4)

A dish that was thrust down one's throat at college, both as a waiter (learning front-of-house skills) and on the few occasions we had a cookery lesson, was Choufleur Polonaise – a cauliflower dish (very trendy, 20 odd years ago). More recently in Italy I enjoyed a similar dish of macaroni, breadcrumbs and cauliflower, and I thought with the addition of hard-boiled egg, parsley and Parmesan it was going to be a great pasta. So here it is, and I've dedicated it to my old college. Follow that with baked peaches with amaretti biscuits, a classic Italian number.

Westminster Cauli Pasta

8 oz (225 g) mini cauliflower florets
salt and ground black pepper
12 oz (350 g) macaroni
3 oz (75 g) unsalted butter
2 oz (50 g) dry natural breadcrumbs
2 tbsp chopped flat parsley leaves
3 hard-boiled eggs, chopped
4 tbsp freshly grated Parmesan

Cook the cauliflower florets in plenty of boiling salted water for 2 minutes. Remove with a slotted spoon and keep warm. In the same water, cook the pasta until *al dente*. While the pasta is cooking, heat the butter in a frying pan, add the breadcrumbs and fry until golden. Combine the breadcrumbs with the cauliflower, parsley and hard-boiled egg. Drain the pasta and combine with the cauliflower mix. Season to taste, top with Parmesan, toss once more, and serve with a leaf salad.

Baked Amaretti Peaches

12 amaretti biscuits
2 tbsp amaretto liqueur
2 oz (50 g) unsalted butter, softened
4 large fresh peaches, preferably white
¾ pint (450 ml) sweet white wine
Mascarpone cheese (optional)

Preheat the oven to 200°C/400°F/Gas 6. Crush the amaretti biscuits with a rolling pin. Mix the biscuit crumbs with the liqueur and the butter. Split the peaches in two and discard the stone; peel the peaches if desired but it is unnecessary. Place a spoonful of the biscuit mixture in the centre of each peach half. Place the peaches cut-side up in a shallow baking dish, pouring the wine into the bottom of the dish. Cook for about 20 minutes at the high temperature above or 35 minutes at 180°C/350°F/Gas 4. Serve with a dollop of Mascarpone if required. Dribble the peaches with any remaining cooking liquor.

HEALTH, COMFORT AND CRUDITÉS

(SERVES 4)

On my travels I've always enjoyed melting a huge Raclette cheese in front of the fire and scraping the oozings on to wonderful Belle de Fontaine potatoes, with a little rock salt, a few cornichons (gherkins), and not much else save a good glass of red wine. Often the Swiss have electric braziers that serve the same purpose. So that idea forms the main course. To start, just a few crudités with some tapénade, and you're in a healthy heaven. We must compromise on the cheese as few of us have log fires or electric braziers, so it's charcuterie with melted cheese and creamy new potatoes.

Crudités with Tapénade

Use any of the following as the crudités:
clean button mushrooms, quartered
broccoli florets
cauliflower florets
baby carrots
cucumber batons
radishes
spring onions
chicory leaves
cherry tomatoes
sugar snap peas
red or yellow peppers
Black Olive Paste (see page 131)

Wash and arrange the vegetables around a cabbage with a hollowed-out centre. Use this as a receptacle for the tapénade (or Black Olive Paste). Dip at leisure.

Cheesy Potatoes with Charcuterie

1½ lb (675 g) Belle de Fontaine new potatoes (or any other waxy variety)
4 oz (100 g) unsalted butter
1 tbsp extra virgin olive oil
3 cloves garlic, cut into slivers
1 tsp soft thyme leaves
rock salt and ground black pepper
7 oz (200 g) Raclette, Taleggio or Reblochon cheese
cornichons (small gherkins)
10 oz (250 g) mixed salamis, Parma ham etc.

Wash and thinly slice the potatoes. In a heavy frying pan with a lid, heat the butter and olive oil and cook the garlic and thyme over a medium heat for 5 minutes. Arrange the potatoes in the pan, cover with a lid, and cook for about 15 minutes or until the potatoes are soft. Season with salt and ground black pepper. Thinly slice the cheese, place on top of the potatoes and cook for a further 3 minutes until the cheese has melted; alternatively place the pan under the grill and melt the cheese this way. Serve from the pan so that the mixture keeps hot and the cheese doesn't become rubbery. Serve with a bowl of cornichons, another of rock salt, and a plate of charcuterie.

SAVOURIES REVISITED

(SERVES 2-4 DEPENDING ON YOUR APPETITE)

Since I opened my first British/Irish restaurant, The Atrium on Millbank, I've discovered the pleasures of the savoury — long forgotten on British menus. I can't imagine why it took me so long to realise that these shores of ours have so much to offer in the way of forgotten foods. The dishes on this page are not so much a menu, more an introduction to the delights of the savoury.

Cod's Roe Savoury

8 oz (225 g) cod's roe
2 oz (50 g) cod's liver (optional)
salt and ground black pepper
2 oz (50 g) unsalted butter
1 tbsp chopped onion
1 tbsp chopped parsley
1½ tsp anchovy essence
½ tsp English mustard
2 slices white country bread

Boil the cod's roe and liver in salted water. While this is cooking, melt half the butter and cook the onion until soft but not brown. Drain the roe and liver and chop fine; add them to the softened onion. Cook for 3 minutes, then add the parsley, anchovy essence and English mustard. Season with ground black pepper. Toast the bread, liberally butter each slice, and pile high with the savoury mix.

Scrambled Crab

4 oz (100 g) white crab meat
4 eggs, lightly beaten
salt and ground black pepper
2 slices wholemeal bread
3 oz (75 g) unsalted butter
2 tbsp double cream

Combine the crab with the beaten eggs. Season with salt and ground black pepper. Toast the bread, and spread with 1 oz (25 g) of the butter. Keep warm. Heat the remaining butter in a non-stick frying pan, pour in the eggs and stir until cooked enough for your fancy. Fold in the double cream and spoon on to the buttered toast.

Hot Cheese Pudding

6 slices bread, crustless, cut in triangles
unsalted butter
3 eggs
1 tsp Worcestershire sauce
1 tsp Dijon mustard
¼ pint (150 ml) double cream
salt and ground white pepper
4 oz (100 g) Gruyère or
Cheddar cheese, grated

Preheat the oven to 180°/350°F/Gas 4. Butter both sides of each bread triangle. Line four ramekins with the triangles. Beat the egg with the Worcestershire sauce, mustard and cream. Season to taste. Add the cheese. Pour into the ramekins and cook in a warm water bath in the oven for 20 minutes.

FANCY A FRY-UP?

(SERVES 4)

Prawn toast must be the No. 1 bestseller in Chinese restaurants. The prawns are puréed with pork fat; I bet you didn't know that, but it's a fact. I make a dish with minced raw prawns, heavily seasoned, and made into the shape of cutlets, deeply popular with children. I'm going to follow that with some apple fritters with rum and clotted cream.

Prawn Cutlets

2 slices bread, crusts removed
¼ pint (150 ml) unsweetened coconut milk
1 lb (450 g) shelled jumbo uncooked prawns
1 onion, chopped
½ tsp salt
2 chillies, finely diced
½ tsp grated ginger
pinch saffron, soaked in 1 tbsp warm water
2 eggs, beaten
1 tsp chopped mint leaves
1 tsp chopped coriander leaves
salt and ground black pepper
breadcrumbs
vegetable oil for frying

Soak the bread slices in the coconut milk. Squeeze to remove most of the milk. Put the bread in the bowl of a food processor with the prawns, onion, salt, chillies, ginger, saffron and eggs. Process to a fine purée, then and add the herbs and seasoning. Remove from the processor and shape the mix into four cutlets. Coat the cutlets in bread crumbs and fry in oil until golden on both sides. Drain well on absorbent kitchen paper. Serve with a leaf salad and noodles or new potatoes.

Apple Fritters

4 oz (100 g) plain flour
1 tbsp melted butter
1 egg yolk
1 tbsp caster sugar
grated peel of ½ lemon
3 tbsp water
rum
½ tsp salt
2 egg whites, beaten until stiff
1 lb (450 g) Cox's apples, peeled
vegetable oil for frying
icing sugar for dusting

Make a batter by beating together the flour, butter, egg yolk, sugar, lemon peel, water, 2 tbsp rum and the salt. Allow to stand for up to half an hour. Just before use, fold in the beaten egg whites. Cut each apple into six wedges, removing the core. Dip each wedge into the batter and fry a few at a time, in deep hot oil. Repeat until all are fried. Drain well on absorbent kitchen paper. Sprinkle the fritters with a little rum and dust with icing sugar.

Macaroni with Garlic, Eggs and Bacon

Sexy Toffee Pudding

SUBTLE IMPERSONATIONS
(SERVES 2)

The French have their version of pizza which they call pissaladière (who called which first, I wonder?), which has a topping of onions, anchovies, olives and tomatoes. We haven't time for that, but why not use the same delicious topping on toast? It's one of those dishes that's been around for yonks, but seems to have lost its fashion status. I call the main course Sort of Stroganoff because I'd hate to offend the originator with this bastardised version. Good nosh all the same.

Pissaladière Toast

2 onions, finely sliced
1 clove garlic, finely diced
2 tsp thyme leaves
good olive oil
2 tomatoes, seeded and diced
1 tbsp stoned black olives, diced
8 canned anchovy fillets, chopped
balsamic vinegar
ground black pepper
2 slices country bread

Cook the onions, garlic and thyme leaves in 2 tbsp of the olive oil until the onions are soft but not brown. Add the tomatoes, olives and anchovies and combine well. Season with a dash of balsamic vinegar and plenty of black pepper. Dribble the slices of bread with a little olive oil and chargrill or grill. Top with the onion mixture and serve immediately.

A Sort of Stroganoff

6 oz (175 g) fettucine or egg noodles
salt and ground black pepper
2 oz (50 g) unsalted butter
8 oz (225 g) beef fillet tail, cut into
½-in (1-cm) strips
plain flour
1 tbsp olive oil
½ onion, finely diced
3 oz (75 g) clean button mushrooms, sliced
3 fl oz (85 ml) red wine
dash Worcestershire sauce
1 tsp Dijon mustard
1 tsp paprika
¼ pint (150 ml) soured cream
dash brandy or dry sherry

Cook the noodles in boiling salted water, then drain and toss with half the butter and ground black pepper. Keep warm. While the noodles are cooking, toss the beef in seasoned flour, then flash-fry the strips in the remaining hot butter and the oil until brown but still rare. Remove the beef from the pan and set aside. In the same pan, cook the onion and mushrooms until soft but not brown. Pour in the red wine and bring to the boil, scraping all the grungy bits from the bottom of the pan. Add a dash of Worcestershire, the mustard and the paprika; stir to combine. Return the meat to the pan with the soured cream and warm through. Finish the sauce with a dash of brandy or sherry and season with salt and ground black pepper. Serve immediately with the buttered noodles.

SOURCING THE SAUCE

(SERVES 4)

This menu isn't really a menu at all, but a selection of bits and bobs that will go admirably with certain dishes. All can be made in advance and kept for at least one week.

Sweet and Sour Dipping Sauce

4 tbsp caster sugar
3 tbsp rice vinegar
2 tbsp Heinz tomato ketchup
2 tsp soy sauce
¼ pint (150 ml) water
2 tbsp corn oil
3 tsp finely chopped garlic
2 tsp finely chopped ginger
2 tsp cornflour dissolved in 2 tbsp cold water
6 spring onions, sliced
salt and ground black pepper

Dissolve the sugar in the vinegar, ketchup, soy and water. Heat the corn oil, add the garlic and ginger, and stir-fry for 30 seconds. Add the combined liquids, bring to the boil, reduce heat and stir in the cornflour mix. Stir for a further 30 seconds and fold in the spring onions. Season to taste and serve warm. The sauce can be reheated if you wish to make it in advance. Use with Chinese fried foods .

Coriander-mint Chutney

2oz (50 g) mint leaves
3oz (75 g) coriander leaves
1 onion, roughly chopped
1 in (2.5 cm) fresh ginger, peeled and chopped
1 chilli, roughly chopped
½ tsp cumin seeds
1 clove garlic
1 tsp salt
2 tsp lemon juice
1 tbsp desiccated coconut, moistened in a little water

Blend all the ingredients in a food processor until smooth, and store in an airtight container in the refrigerator. This makes an excellent dip if you fold a little into some yogurt to your taste. Eat with poppadoms and tandoori dishes.

Oriental Mustard Sauce

¼ pint (150 ml) Dijon mustard
¼ pint (150 ml) sesame oil
2 tbsp rice vinegar
1 tbsp dry sherry or mirin (a Japanese sweet wine)
2 tbsp chopped spring onion
3 tbsp chopped coriander leaves
salt and ground black pepper

Blend the first four ingredients in a food processor until thoroughly combined. Tip into an airtight container and fold in the spring onion and coriander. Season to taste and store in the refrigerator. Use with fish and white meat.

MOUNTAIN MAGIC

(SERVES 4)

I've recently learnt how to ski – pretty daunting at forty something, but I couldn't let my kids show up my macho image for what it really is. Anyway, even if my limbs didn't quite match up to the messages my brain was transmitting, I knew one thing, I didn't intend to put up with second-rate food. To start, I deadened the pain with more than adequate supplies of an interpretation of Mulled Wine or Glogg. Then, once my body was suitably impressed with this liquid sustenance, it was time to start dipping into a bubbling pot of Cheese Fondue. If you haven't got a fondue set then just melt a chunk of Raclette in front of the fire, scrape off the melted cheese and serve with bread or potatoes.

Hot Spiced Wine

10 oz (275 g) caster sugar
1 pint (600 ml) water
grated rind of 1 orange and 1 lemon
10 cloves
1 stick cinnamon
grating of nutmeg
8 cardamom pods
2 bottles red wine
6 tbsp brandy-soaked sultanas

Melt the sugar in the water. Add the remainder of the ingredients except the sultanas and simmer for 20 minutes. Do not allow to boil. Strain the wine into toddy glasses each containing a few brandy-soaked sultanas. Enjoy.

Cheese Fondue

1 clove garlic, cut in 2
12 fl oz (350 ml) dry white wine or cider
1 tsp lemon juice
12 oz (350 g) Emmenthal cheese, grated
8 oz (225 g) Beaufort cheese, cut in flakes
2 tsp cornflour
3 fl oz (85 ml) Kirsch
salt, ground black pepper and grated nutmeg
a bowl of bite-sized pieces of baguette
a bowl of hot new potatoes in their skins
gherkins and baby onions

Rub a fondue dish or saucepan with the garlic. Put the wine or cider and lemon juice into the pan and heat gently. When the liquid bubbles, add the cheeses and stir continuously until melted. Place the pan on top of the fondue heater. Dissolve the cornflour in the Kirsch and, when the cheese mix is creamy, stir it in. Beat vigorously for a few minutes and season with salt, pepper and a little grated nutmeg. Let everyone start dipping their bread and potatoes into the mix, and serve with baby gherkins and onions. If you lose your bread or potato in the cheese then it's time to play 'strip-fondue': as a forfeit, you have to remove one item of clothing, which adds a little more spice to the evening's activities.

GARLIC MISCHIEF

(SERVES 2)

It's the run-up to Christmas. These can be stressful times. It's cold outside, yet the shops can be cauldrons of chaos, packed with truck-loads of dithering, dutiful disciples, lingering over what to buy their loved ones. Me, I'm an impulsive Taurean. I see, I buy, I'm out, but how do I fight my way through the crowds? Answer: an early morning lunch supping on garlic soup followed by a steaming bowl of equally garlicky mussels. Garlic is good for you, but it can be anti-social; miraculously, it will help you clear a path through the crowds and be first every time at the checkout!

A Warming Garlic Soup

5 cloves garlic, thinly sliced
2 oz (50 g) pancetta or streaky bacon, finely diced
1 red chilli, finely sliced
1 tsp soft thyme leaves
2 fl oz (50 ml) olive oil
4 thick slices country bread, crusts removed
½ tsp paprika
1 pint (600 ml) chicken stock
salt and ground black pepper

In a saucepan, cook the garlic, pancetta, chilli and thyme in the olive oil until golden. Break the bread into small cubes and add to the pan with the paprika and chicken stock. Bring to the boil and simmer for 10 minutes, stirring from time to time until the bread has broken down and thickened the liquid. Season to taste.

A Bowl of Steaming Mussels

2 fl oz (50 ml) olive oil
1 onion, finely diced
4 canned anchovy fillets, chopped
4 large cloves garlic, chopped
1 red chilli, chopped
½ pint (300 ml) dry white wine
3 lb (1.4 kg) clean mussels
4 tbsp finely chopped parsley
ground black pepper

Heat the olive oil in a large saucepan over a medium heat. Add the onion, anchovy, garlic and chilli; cook until soft but not brown. Add the wine and bring to the boil. Simmer for 5 minutes, then add the mussels and cover. Increase the heat and cook for approximately 5 minutes, shaking the pan from time to time. Remove the mussels with a slotted spoon to two warm bowls, discarding any that have not opened. Boil the remaining liquor for a further 2 minutes, then add the parsley and season with ground black pepper. Pour over the mussels. Serve with crusty bread or a bowl of salted *frites*.

CHRISTMAS EVE COMFORT
(SERVES 2)

It's Christmas Eve — or it soon will be. You've prepared everything for the big day and now you're shattered. It's time for your partner to give you a helping of the 'cuddle factor'; feet up, a big drink, and total relaxation while he/she knocks up a little supper and then proceeds to pamper you for the remainder of the evening. I suggest it's kept simple with a few wonderful scallops on a hot potato salad, followed by a savoury cheese number inspired by Glamorgan sausages.

Scallops with Hot Potato Salad

8 oz (225 g) new potatoes, washed
4 tbsp extra virgin olive oil
1 shallot, finely diced
2 tomatoes, seeded and diced
6 basil leaves, ripped
2 tbsp mixed chives and tarragon
6 diver-caught scallops, shucked
juice of a lemon

Cook the new potatoes until tender in boiling salted water, then slice and keep warm. Heat the olive oil in a saucepan, add the shallot and cook over a low heat until soft. Add the potatoes, tomatoes and herbs and keep warm. Put a teaspoon of the olive oil in a non-stick frying pan and fry the scallops for 1 minute on each side until golden. Season the potato salad with salt, plenty of ground black pepper and lemon juice. Serve with the scallops.

Savoury Cheese Sausages

2 egg yolks
1 tbsp snipped chives
1 tsp chopped parsley
½ tsp mustard powder
4 oz (100 g) fresh white breadcrumbs
3 oz (75 g) Caerphilly cheese, grated
salt and black pepper
2 egg whites,
beaten butter for frying

In a food processor, combine the egg yolks, herbs, mustard and half the breadcrumbs. Add the cheese and pulse to combine, then season. Roll the mixture into 2-in (5 cm) sausages; dip them in egg white and then in the remaining breadcrumbs. Fry in butter until golden brown. Serve with a green tomato chutney.

CHRISTMAS CHEER

(SERVES 8)

Midnight Mass on Christmas Eve is one of the few occasions apart from weddings and funerals when our churches get a good turnout. St Martin's in the Fields in Trafalgar Square where I used to sing is booked up weeks in advance. Given that the weather is usually pretty cold and the church can be even colder, a hot alcoholic flask works a treat; a little sacrilegious I know, so if that's against the rules then participate afterwards in a steaming glass of 'Christmas Spirit' accompanied by a warming croissant stuffed with bacon, mushrooms and cheese.

Christmas Spirit

1 bottle cognac
2 oz (50 g) caster sugar
rind of 1 orange stuck with 6 cloves
4 cardamom seeds
2-in (5-cm) stick cinnamon
2 oz (50 g) raisins, soaked in some of the cognac
2 oz (50 g) unsalted flaked almonds
½ pint (300 ml) dry sherry

Heat all the ingredients except for the sherry in a non-reactive saucepan. Flame the liquid if desired, but with caution. Stir until hot and the sugar has dissolved, then add the sherry. Serve piping hot into glasses with a few almonds in the bottom.

Bacon Croissant Buttie

2 onions, sliced
1 tsp soft thyme leaves
2 oz (50 g) unsalted butter
4 oz (100 g) button mushrooms, sliced
salt and ground black pepper
8 slices back bacon, rind removed
8 croissants
Dijon mustard
4 oz (100 g) Gruyère or Cheddar cheese, grated

Preheat the oven to 180°C/350F/Gas 4. Cook the onion and thyme leaves in the butter until soft but not brown. Add the mushrooms and cook for 5 minutes. Season. In a separate frying pan, or under the grill, cook the bacon until crispy. Meanwhile, cut the croissants three-quarters of the way through and spread with mustard. Place the mushroom mixture on the bottom halves of each croissant. Top with the bacon, then scatter with the grated cheese and place in the oven until the cheese melts.

Other little treats that always go down a storm late on this evening could be warm mince pies with clotted cream, a big bowl of nuts to crack by the fire, hot buttered crumpets with maple syrup and crispy bacon and warm griddle cakes with melting Camembert and cranberry relish.

CHILLING ON BOXING DAY

(SERVES 4)

It's December 26th and the world is waking to the sound of 'plink, plink, fizz'. It's Alka-Seltzer's big day. Heads are throbbing, stomachs groaning; aren't you pleased it's all over for another year? Traditionally Boxing Day is for visiting relatives or going to house parties, but this year why not chill out, curl up in front of the fire, watch a video and eat when you're ready – 4 pm, 5 pm, who cares? Make this a 'nothing' day, and enjoy stress-free eating by kicking off with a 'simple' Caesar Salad, followed by your second Christmas lunch in a sandwich.

Simple Caesar Salad

2oz (50 g) canned anchovy fillets, drained and chopped
¼ pint (150 ml) mayonnaise
1 tbsp cider vinegar
1 tbsp ripped basil leaves
2 cloves garlic, crushed with a little salt
milk
2 small romaine or cos lettuces, leaves torn
1 egg yolk
4 tbsp grated Parmesan
salt and ground black pepper
garlic croûtons

Mash the anchovies with the mayonnaise, then add the vinegar, basil and garlic. Thin down, if required, with a little milk. Mix the lettuce leaves with the dressing, add the egg yolk and toss lightly. Add the remaining ingredients and mix, seasoning to taste.

Christmas Lunch Club Sandwich

12 slices country bread
unsalted butter
turkey stuffing
cranberry sauce
brown and white turkey meat
turkey gravy
baked ham, sliced
tomatoes, sliced
mayonnaise
salt and ground black pepper

Spread the bread with butter. Lay four slices on a work surface, butter-side up; top with a layer of stuffing, then a layer of cranberry sauce, followed by the turkey meat. Spread the turkey with cold gravy, top with another slice of bread, then layers of ham, tomato and mayonnaise. Season, and top with the final slice of bread butter-side down. Serve with McCoys plain crisps. Don't use a knife and fork, just seize in both hands and wrap your laughing gear around a yummy, moreish mouthful.

CALORIE COUNTDOWN TO CHRISTMAS

(SERVES 4)

You can't tell me you don't overeat at Christmas; we all do. It's only saints and angels who have the ability to hold back on their intake, and I don't know many of them. So you have two choices: a self-imposed purge after the New Year festivities (I usually survive until January 3rd), or a cut-back in fats and calories in the run-up to Christmas. This menu is a flimsy gesture, but it's the thought that counts. I'm starting with a little Mushroom Caviar which can be spread on very thin slimming crackers, then some spicy jumbo prawns with a cucumber salad.

Mushroom Caviar

1 tbsp olive oil
½ onion, finely diced
2 cloves garlic, finely diced
1 tsp soft thyme leaves
8 oz (225 g) field mushrooms, roughly chopped
1 tbsp balsamic vinegar
salt and ground black pepper

Heat the oil in a deep saucepan over a medium heat. Add the onion, garlic and thyme; cook until soft but not brown. Add the mushrooms, stir to combine, and increase the heat. Cook for 10 minutes, then add the balsamic vinegar and cook until all the liquor has evaporated. Season to taste. Blend the mixture in a food processor until roughly chopped but not pulverised. Serve warm or at room temperature with bread or biscuits.

Spicy Shrimp and Cucumber

1½ lb (675 g) jumbo uncooked prawns, shell on
1 onion, roughly cut
1 bunch coriander, chopped
2 cloves garlic, finely chopped
1 tsp ground cumin
1 tsp ground coriander
3 chillies, finely chopped
salt and ground black pepper
1 cucumber, peeled and roughly chopped
4 tbsp low-fat plain yogurt
1 tbsp lemon juice
2 plum tomatoes, seeded and roughly cut

Fill the bottom of a steamer with salted water and bring to the boil. Combine the prawns with the onion, half the fresh coriander, the garlic, cumin, ground coriander, half the chilies and a teaspoons of ground black pepper. Set aside. Combine the cucumber with the remainder of the chopped coriander and chilli. Mix together the yogurt, lemon juice and the tomato, and mix into the cucumber. Season to taste. Place the prawns in the top part of the steamer, place over the boiling water, cover and cook for 4 minutes. Serve with the cucumber salad on the side.

TIME TO BE INDULGENT

(SERVES 4–6)

There are days when I can only be satisfied by scoffing an ounce or two of caviar. It's the ultimate in self-indulgence, blowing away the post-Christmas cobwebs, turning grey days blue, and adding a little wickedness to my innocent world. Purists need no adornments, except perhaps a blini or two. I, myself, enjoy caviar in any form, so here I include an easy blini recipe, a Caviar Dip, and the ultimate experience: Baked New Potatoes with Caviar and soured cream.

Buckwheat Blinis

½ pint (300 ml) milk
½ oz (15 g) fresh yeast, crumbled
4 eggs, separated
½ tsp salt
1 tsp caster sugar
9 oz (250 g) buckwheat flour
3 oz (75 g) unsalted butter, melted
butter for frying

Scald the milk and allow to cool to lukewarm. Add the yeast and stir to soften. Beat the egg yolks until thick. Add the yeast mixture to the egg yolks, then fold in the remaining ingredients except for the egg whites and butter. Allow to rest for 15 minutes. Beat the egg whites until stiff and fold into the mixture. Butter a non-stick pan and cook individual tablespoons of the batter until golden brown, turning once. Serve the blinis warm with melted butter, caviar, lemon, soured cream and fine dice of onion.

Caviar Dip

10 oz (275 g) Greek yogurt
1 tsp creamed horseradish
1 tbsp chopped parsley
2 tsp grated onion and juice
1 tsp Colman's English mustard
2 oz (50 g) caviar

Combine all the ingredients except the caviar. Carefully fold in the caviar without bursting too many of the 'eggs'. Serve with hot roasted 'soldiers' or crisp raw vegetables

Baked New Potatoes with Caviar

1lb (450 g) new potatoes, washed
rock salt and ground black pepper
½ pint (300 ml) thick soured cream
1 oz (25 g) caviar
1 bunch chives, snipped

Preheat oven to 200°C/400°F/Gas 6. Place the new potatoes on the rock salt in a baking dish. Pop the dish into the oven and bake until the potato skins are crisp and the centres fluffy. Cut an X in each potato and squeeze gently. Top each potato with a dollop of soured cream and ½ tsp caviar; sprinkle with chives and ground black pepper. Serve immediately.

TALKING SOUFFLE SENSE

(SERVES 2–4)

It's another year, resolution time; it's time to get serious about your cooking. You're going to prepare a soufflé. Shock, horror, I can hear you say, but you mustn't. Soufflés need a little confidence and not many cooking skills. This Cheese and Bacon Soufflé is more substantial than the usual cloud-like affair, but it's good and you don't have to whip any egg whites. To start, one of those savoury dishes usually associated with kids but loved by big kids too: Creamy Sardines on Toast. This menu extravaganza may take a smidgen over 30 minutes, but it's worth it.

Creamy Sardines on Toast

4 oz (100 g) unsalted butter
½ onion, finely diced
1 tsp soft thyme leaves
6 tbsp soft white breadcrumbs
¾ pint (450 ml) double cream
2 small cans sardines, drained and mashed
3 hard-boiled eggs, chopped
salt and ground black pepper
toast

Melt the butter over a medium heat. Add the onion and thyme and cook until soft but not brown. Add the remaining ingredients and warm through, stirring to combine. Season to taste. Share the mixture equally between four slices of buttered toast. Pop under a hot grill until bubbling.

Cheese and Bacon Soufflé

3oz (75 g) unsalted butter
3oz (75 g) streaky bacon, diced
½ onion, finely diced
2 oz (50 g) plain flour
½ pint hot milk
salt and cayenne pepper
3 oz (75 g) grated parmesan
4 eggs, well beaten

Preheat the oven to 200°C/400°F/Gas 6. Melt 2oz (50 g) of the butter in a saucepan. With the remainder, butter a soufflé dish. To the butter in the saucepan add the bacon and onion and cook until the onion is soft. Add the flour and stir until combined. Cook for a further 3 minutes, stirring from time to time. Slowly add the milk, stirring constantly for 3 minutes until smooth and thick. Season and add the cheese. Add 4 tbsp of this sauce to the beaten eggs, then return this mixture to the sauce. Combine thoroughly. Pour into the soufflé dish and place in a tray of hot water in the oven. Bake for approximately 20 minutes or until set.

SAFE FROM THE SALES

(SERVES 4)

Are you a masochist? Yes, well then you'll have fun at the sales. For the remainder of us, sales are a turgid experience causing serious stress. After the battle you need to enjoy a care-free eating experience.

Mozzarella Skewers with Black Olive Paste

10 oz (275 g) buffalo Mozzarella
2 tsp soft thyme leaves
salt and freshly ground black pepper
20 slices pancetta or streaky bacon
20 button mushrooms
plain flour for dusting
2 eggs, beaten
fresh breadcrumbs
4 tbsp melted butter
Black Olive Paste (see below)

Cut the Mozzarella into twenty cubes and season with thyme, salt and pepper. Wrap each cube in the pancetta and thread five cubes on to each of four wooden skewers, alternating each cube with a mushroom. Roll the skewers in flour, dip in the egg and then coat with breadcrumbs. Refrigerate until ready to cook. When you return from your shopping expedition, heat the oven to 190°C/375°F/Gas 5. Baste the skewers with melted butter and cook for about 10 minutes or until golden and the cheese is starting to melt. Serve with some Black Olive Paste, a salad or a few new potatoes.

Black Olive Paste

8 oz (225 g) stoned black olives
2½ fl oz (75 ml) extra virgin olive oil
2 cloves garlic, finely chopped
⅛ tsp red chilli flakes
½ tsp ground black pepper
1 tbsp capers
grated zest and juice of 1 lemon
pinch salt
1 tbsp chopped Parsley

Blend all the ingredients in a food processor until smooth, or you may prefer to leave it slightly chunky.

A Cup of Something Hot

½ pint (300 ml) water
3 tsp unsweetened cocoa powder
3 tbsp caster sugar
2 oz (50 g) plain chocolate
½ pint (300 ml) milk
½ pint (300 ml) brewed espresso or strong coffee
whipped cream

In a bowl whisk together the water, cocoa and sugar. Transfer to a saucepan and add the chocolate, milk and coffee. Whisk over a medium heat until the liquid is hot and frothy, about 10 minutes. Serve hot, topped with whipped cream.

THINKING SLIM

(SERVES 4)

Christmas is but a memory; however, expanded stomachs are a fact! For most of you it is back to grey January days with noses to the grindstone. This is the time I fly to Southern Australia to see my kids, where the temperature is 35° and the beers are 5°. I take advantage of these slimming temperatures to eat healthily. How about Asparagus with Red Pepper Sauce (125 calories), followed by Baked Cod with Olives and Spring Onions (280 calories) to relieve you of the waist-line pressure.

Asparagus with Red Pepper Sauce

salt and ground black pepper
4 red peppers, seeded and roughly chopped
1 onion, roughly chopped
2 cloves garlic, crushed with a little salt
1 red chilli, finely diced
12 leaves basil
1 tbsp walnut oil
1 tbsp sherry vinegar
1 tbsp lemon juice
1½ lb (675 g) trimmed asparagus
ground black pepper

Bring a pan of salted water to the boil. Place all the ingredients except for the asparagus in a separate large, non-reactive saucepan, cover, and simmer for 20 minutes. Pour the softened mixture into a food processor and blend until smooth; season and pass through a fine sieve and set aside. When ready to eat, cook the asparagus in the boiling water for 6 minutes, then drain. Spoon the red pepper sauce (hot or cold) on to four plates and top with the asparagus. Garnish with ripped basil leaves and grindings of black pepper.

Baked Cod with Olives and Spring Onions

1 tsp extra virgin olive oil
4 x 6-oz (175-g) cod fillets
16 stoned black olives, chopped
3 tbsp chopped parsley
2 tbsp chopped dill
2 bunches spring onions, finely sliced
2 chillies, finely diced
juice of 2 limes
salt and ground black pepper
½ pint (300 ml) tomato juice

Preheat the oven to 230°C/450°F/Gas 8. Lightly oil a baking dish and place the cod in the bottom. Top each fillet with a mixture of olives, herbs, spring onions and chillies; dribble with the lime juice. Season, then pour the tomato juice around the fish and bring to the boil over a medium heat. Place the dish in the oven and cook for 10 minutes. Serve immediately, using the juices as a sauce, along with a herbed leaf salad.

RAIDING THE PANTRY

(SERVES 4)

The store cupboard is vital to my very existence. Don't you find there are times when you can't be bothered to go to the shops; that's when you fall back on to a treasure trove of tins, packets, spices and (dare I say it?) stock cubes. Assuming that most households have essentials such as garlic, onions, eggs and bacon, how about a warming soup of tomatoes and flageolet beans, followed by macaroni with garlic, eggs and bacon.

Tomato and Flageolet Bean Soup

1 onion, finely diced
2 cloves garlic, finely diced
pinch dried chilli flakes
2 oz (50 g) unsalted butter
1 x 375-g can chopped tomatoes
with basil
2 vegetable stock cubes
1 sachet bouquet garni
1 x 375-g can flageolet beans, drained
salt and ground black pepper
1 tbsp pesto
1 tbsp extra virgin olive oil

In a saucepan, pan-fry the onion, garlic and chilli flakes in the butter until soft but without colour. Add the tomatoes, 1¾ pints (1 litre) boiling water, the stock cubes and bouquet garni; simmer for 15 minutes. Fold in the beans, bring back to simmering temperature and season to taste. Serve in four warm soup bowls, topped with a little pesto and a dribble of olive oil, accompanied by hot crusty bread.

Macaroni with Garlic, Eggs and Bacon

1 lb (450 g) macaroni
olive oil
4 slices streaky bacon, cut in strips
3 cloves garlic, finely diced
1 onion, finely diced
pinch chilli flakes
1 tbsp extra virgin olive oil
4 x 7-minute boiled eggs, peeled
4 tbsp grated Parmesan

Cook the macaroni in boiling salted water with a little olive oil. Meanwhile, pan-fry the bacon, garlic, onion and chilli flakes in the extra virgin olive oil until the onion is soft but without colour. Separate the egg whites from the yolks. Chop the whites and add to the bacon mixture. Mash the yolks to a smooth paste with a little water. When the macaroni has cooked, drain well and add to the bacon mixture. Tip in the egg yolk paste and mix to combine. Garnish with hardboiled eggs and serve immediately with the Parmesan.

TAKING CHEESE TO HEART

(SERVES 4)

Cheese has a role to play in all our lives – not a huge role, but a role all the same. If food had star signs, then cheese would be a Gemini as it has a split personality; on the one hand we are told to cut back on dairy products, on the other 'dairy products are invaluable because of their calcium content'. I have a simple rule: if you like it, eat it. So I suggest this menu is kept for National Cheese Day. To start, a delicious warming Cheese Soup, to follow, Saltimbocca, using pork instead of veal.

Cheese Soup

2 onions, finely diced
3 cloves garlic, finely diced
1 sprig thyme
1 bay leaf
2 oz (50 g) unsalted butter
3 tbsp plain flour
4 tbsp dry white wine
1½ pint (900 ml) chicken stock
½ pint (300 ml) double cream
8 oz (225 g) Roquefort cheese, crumbled
4 oz (100 g) Cheddar cheese, crumbled
salt and ground black pepper
1 tbsp snipped chives

Cook the onion, garlic, thyme and bay leaf gently in the butter for approximately 10 minutes. Add the flour and combine well, cooking for a further 2 minutes. Add the wine and chicken stock and bring to the boil stirring continuously. Reduce the heat and simmer for a further 10 minutes. Remove from the heat and whisk in the cream and the cheeses. Pour the soup into a food processor or liquidiser and blend until smooth. Return to the saucepan and heat the soup to just under boiling. Season to taste and garnish with the chives. Serve immediately.

Saltimbocca

4 large scallops of pork, pounded thin
8 thin slices Parma ham, rind removed
8 thin slices buffalo Mozzarella
16 sage leaves, finely chopped
4 tsp freshly grated Parmesan
4 oz (100 g) unsalted butter
¼ pint (150 ml) dry white wine
salt and ground black pepper

Lay the pork scallops on a cutting board and top each with a slice of Parma ham, followed by two slices of Mozzarella, a sprinkling of sage and Parmesan, and another slice of Parma ham, in that order. Melt ½ oz (15 g) of the butter in a heavy frying pan and fry two of the pork escalopes, plain-side down, for 2 minutes. Add another ½ oz (15 g) of the butter, flip the pork over and cook, Parma ham-side down, for a further 2 minutes. Remove from the pan and keep warm. Repeat this exercise with the remaining pork escalopes. Keep warm. In the same pan, add the remaining sage and the dry white wine. Over a fierce heat boil the sauce for 1 minute. Add the remaining butter and whisk until blended, then season to taste. Pour the sauce over the pork and serve immediately with a leaf salad.

NOT COMING HOME TO REALITY

(SERVES 4)

I'm sure many of you will have had holidays in the Caribbean sun, and those who haven't will be dreaming of going. Much of the food in that region can be unpalatable for our tastes, the staple diet being rice and peas, but when the food is good, it's very very good. How about an offering of two excellent fish dishes, Stamp and Go and Blaff; I haven't a clue why the dishes are called such, but they're fun.

Stamp and Go

8 oz (225 g) salt or fresh cod, flaked
2 spring onions, finely sliced
2 hot chillis, finely diced
1 tsp minced ginger
1 tsp finely chopped garlic
8 oz (225 g) plain flour
1 tsp baking powder
About 4 tbsp cold water
About ½ pint (300 ml) coconut or
vegetable oil

In a bowl mix together the flaked cod (if salted, soak overnight in running water), spring onion, chilli, ginger and garlic. Fold in the flour and baking powder, and add enough water to make a sticky batter; season to taste. Heat the oil to 190°C/375°F in a heavy saucepan or domestic deep-fryer and drop 3-4 dessertspoonfuls of the batter at a time into the oil. Cook until golden, approximately 5 minutes. Serve with your favourite chilli sauce.

Blaff

salt and ground black pepper
8 crushed allspice berries
4 cloves garlic, crushed with a little salt
2 hot chillies, finely chopped
juice of 3 limes
4 red snapper (or other red fish), scaled
and head off
3 pints (1.5 litres) water
1 onion, sliced
1 bouquet garni

Mix the first five ingredients to make a marinade. Place the fish in the marinade for up to 1 hour. When ready to cook, add the marinade to the remaining ingredients and bring to a rolling boil. Add the fish and return to the boil; remove from the heat and allow to rest for 15 minutes. Remove the bouquet garni and serve the fish in bowls, covered with the cooking liquor. Serve with lime wedges and plain boiled rice.

SIMPLE LUXURIES

(SERVES 2)

Christmas and New Year seem light years away, so let's buckle down for the remaining grey winter days. It's hard to motivate yourself when everyone is drifting around with long faces, so dig into some hidden luxuries and put a smile on your partner's face. Creamy scrambled egg with smoked haddock and caviar followed by a melting mozzarella and wild mushroom sandwich.

Eggcetera

2 oz (50 g) unsalted butter
6 oz (150 g) smoked haddock, skinned and diced
6 large eggs, beaten
4 tbsp double cream
good pinch nutmeg
salt and ground black pepper
1 oz (25 g) Sevruga caviar

Heat the butter in a non-stick frying pan until foaming. Add the haddock and cook over a low heat for 3 minutes. Meanwhile, beat the eggs with the cream and nutmeg. Tip the eggs on to the haddock and scramble until barely set. Season to taste. Top the eggs with a dollop of caviar.

Wild Mushroom Sandwich

1 shallot, finely diced
4 oz (100 g) cèpes or button mushrooms, finely sliced
1 tsp soft thyme leaves
unsalted butter
4 thin slices country bread
4 thin slices buffalo Mozzarella
salt and ground black pepper

Pan-fry the shallot, mushrooms and thyme in 1 oz (25 g) of the butter until soft but not brown. Butter the four slices of bread. Lay out two slices and top each with a slice of Mozzarella and some mushrooms: top this with another slice of cheese and the other slice of bread. Season each sandwich and press the bread slices firmly together. Fry in sizzling butter, turning once, until golden on both sides.

CHRISTMAS IS BUT A MEMORY

(SERVES 4)

When you've been hammering yourself, it's time for you to give your body a break. Usually I'll go off the booze for the month of February, but often I'm too busy to tackle such a serious issue .... it's usually 'I'll start tomorrow'. No booze, no meat, just plenty of juices, pasta, vegetables and fruits. I've been practising some vegetable combinations recently and have come up with an easy menu in skewered tofu, onion, mushroom and bok choy followed by Spaghetti with Herby Green Sauce.

Marinated Tofu, Onion, Mushroom and Bok Choy

¼ pint (150 ml) soy sauce
¼ pint (150 ml) fresh orange juice
2 tbsp rice vinegar
2 tbsp sesame oil
1 clove garlic, finely chopped
2 tbsp chopped coriander
2 tbsp finely chopped ginger
½ tsp finely chopped chilli
1 head bok choy, or equivalent in spring greens or spinach
1 lb (450 g) tofu, drained and cut in 1-in (2.5-cm) cubes
20 shiitake or button mushrooms
1 red onion, peeled and cut lengthways into 8

Prepare the marinade by combining the first eight ingredients. Separate the bok choy leaves and remove the stems. Cut them into 1-in (2.5-cm) sections. Roll up the leaves and marinate with the stems, the tofu, mushrooms and onion for up to 1 hour, depending on how strongly flavoured you like your vegetables. Thread the ingredients on to four thick wooden skewers, and cook on a barbie or under a grill for about 12 minutes, basting with the marinade and turning regularly.

Spaghetti with Herby Green Sauce

1 lb (450 g) spaghetti
½ bunch flat parsley, leaves only
2 tbsp chopped gherkins, rinsed
2 tbsp capers, rinsed
2 cloves garlic, chopped
2 tbsp red wine vinegar
¼ pint (150ml) extra virgin olive oil
salt and ground black pepper
grated Parmesan cheese

Cook the spaghetti in plenty of boiling salted water with 1 tbsp of the olive oil until *al dente*, then drain. While the spaghetti is cooking, combine the parsley, gherkins, capers, garlic and red wine vinegar in a food processor until smooth; with the machine still running, add the remaining oil in a thin stream. Season to taste. Toss the spaghetti with the sauce and sprinkle with Parmesan. Serve immediately.

SIMPLY VALENTINE

(SERVES 2)

It's St Valentine's Day, a commercial exercise to jack up the price of red roses. Why we need an excuse to be romantic is beyond me, but for you once-a-year romantics, here's a simple, sexy, scrunching, sucking menu. I suggest you hand-feed your partner with new potatoes topped with soured cream and caviar, followed by native and rock oysters, then poached lobster with warm asparagus and melted butter, followed by a smoochie tub of Haagen-Dazs ice cream.

New Potatoes with Soured Cream and Caviar

8 oz (225 g) new potatoes, cooked in
their skins
4 tbsp soured cream
1oz (25 g) Sevruga caviar
snipped chives

Warm the potatoes, make a cross cut in each, and top with soured cream and caviar. Garnish with chives.

Rock and Native Oysters

6 rock oysters
6 Colchester native oysters
lemon juice

Ask your fishmonger to open the oysters late in the afternoon. No adornments, just a squeeze of lemon, and pour them one – by one – down your partner's throat.

Boiled Lobster with Asparagus

2 x 1½-lb (675-g) live lobsters
10 oz (275 g) jumbo asparagus, woody
stems removed
4 oz (100 g) unsalted butter, melted
rock salt and ground black pepper

Have the fishmonger kill the lobsters. Place them in cold water, salted enough to float a raw egg. Bring to the boil, remove from the heat and leave the lobster in the water for 20 minutes. Meanwhile, cook the asparagus in boiling salted water for 10-12 minutes, depending on their thickness. Drain the lobsters well and cut into suckable-size pieces. Remove the gritty sac from the head and discard. Serve with asparagus, melted butter and plenty of black pepper. Munch, scrunch, investigate, penetrate and eviscerate every little piece.

Haagen-Dazs Ice Cream

1 large tub of your favourite

Open the tub and let their advertisements give you a little inspiration for the rest of the night.

THE MALE VALENTINE

(SERVES 2)

What would the female sex make for dinner on Valentine's Day? The answer, in most cases, would be a 'reservation'. So guys, if you want a romantic session at home, then the cooking is going to be down to you. Cooking is one of the male's sexiest attributes, so start practising if you want to improve your 'pulling power'. How about a simple number to start: Lobster Hearts with Coriander Oil served with a simple salad, followed by a Sexy Toffee Pudding with my favourite caramel ice cream.

Lobster Hearts with Coriander Oil

1 lb (450 g) prepared puff pastry
1 egg yolk, beaten
2 x 1-lb (450-g) lobsters, cooked
1 bunch coriander, leaves only
½ pint extra virgin olive oil
salt and ground black pepper
1 ripe avocado, peeled and mashed
4 oz (100 g) corn niblets
2 tbsp diced red onion
2 tbsp lime juice
2 tbsp Greek yogurt

Preheat the oven to 200°C/400°F/Gas 6. Roll out the pastry to ⅓ in (8 mm) thickness and, with a sharp knife, cut two free-hand hearts about 5 in (13 cm) in length. Brush the top of the pastry with egg yolk, place on a buttered baking sheet and cook in the oven for 20-25 minutes or until golden and cooked. Split the lobsters in two, crack the claws, remove the meat and set aside. Liquidise half the coriander with the olive oil and season to taste. Strain the oil. Chop the remaining coriander and combine with the avocado, corn, red onion, lime juice and yogurt. Split each pastry heart in two horizontally and place a dollop of avocado mixture on the bottom; top with the lobster flesh, a dribble of coriander oil and the pastry top. Serve with a leaf salad and buttered new potatoes.

Sexy Toffee Pudding

4 oz (100 g) butter
3 tbsp golden syrup
4 oz (100 g) soft brown sugar
¼ pint (150 ml) milk, mixed with
¼ pint (150 ml) double cream
6 slices Panettone, cut into 'soldiers'
Ben and Jerry's English Crunchy Toffee
Ice Cream

Preheat the oven to 190°C/375°F/Gas 5. Melt the butter in a saucepan with the golden syrup and sugar. Allow to bubble for 5 minutes. Heat the milk and cream and dip each Panettone soldier into this mixture. Arrange them in a baking dish and, between each layer, dribble a little of the toffee mixture, pouring the remainder over the top. Place in the oven and serve when hot. It can sit in a low oven until the time is right. Serve with the ice cream. Alternatively, forego pudding and serve warm for breakfast the next morning.

A NEW START TO MORNING MUNCHING

(SERVES 6)

I know it's the wrong time of year to be talking on the subject of al fresco breakfasts but, when I was in Australia, eating outside on the 'deck' I enjoyed this terrific home-made muesli. It takes a short time to prepare, so a little pre-planning will be required. This could be followed by a crispy bacon hash. So there you have it, a combination of health and decadence.

Muesli with Bananas and Coconut

¼ pint (150 ml) set honey
¼ pint (150 ml) walnut oil
¼ pint (150 ml) water
6 oz (175 g) oats
2 oz (50 g) sesame seeds
2 oz (50 g) bran flakes
6 oz (175 g) pecan nuts, chopped
2 oz (50 g) desiccated coconut
3 oz (75 g) raisins
3 oz (75 g) flaked almonds
½ pint (300 ml) unsweetened coconut milk, cold
½ pint milk, ice-cold
1 banana, ripe

Preheat the oven to 200°C/400°F/Gas 6. Heat the honey, walnut oil and water; pour over the grains, nuts and dried fruit. Spread out on a non-stick flat roasting tray and roast in the oven until tanned, stirring from time to time so that the grains are well coated with the honey mixture. Remove from the oven and allow to cool. Store in glass jars. When ready to eat, whizz the coconut milk, milk and banana in a blender and pour over the crunchy bits. Top with seasonal fruits; I enjoyed mango and raspberries.

Crispy Bacon Hash

4 slices streaky bacon, diced
1 tbsp olive oil
1 oz (25 g) unsalted butter
1 onion, roughly chopped
2 cooked potatoes, peeled and diced
1 chilli, finely diced
1 clove garlic, finely chopped
1 tsp soft thyme leaves
1 tbsp chopped parsley

In a non-stick pan, cook the bacon until crispy; remove and set aside. Add the oil and butter and cook the onion until soft and slightly caramelised. Add the potato, chilli, garlic and bacon, and cook until the potato is golden, tossing regularly. Season to taste and add the herbs. Serve with poached eggs.

INDEX